Living The ED Principles

Michele Doucette, M. Ed.

Living The ED Principles

Copyright © 2014 by Michele Doucette, St. Clair Publications

All rights reserved. No part of this publication may be reproduced or transmitted in any form or by any means, electronic or mechanical, including photocopying, recording, or by any information storage and retrieval system, without written permission from the author.

ISBN 978-1-935786-72-6

Printed in the United States of America by

St. Clair Publications

PO Box 726

McMinnville, TN 37111-0726

http://stclairpublications.com/

Table of Contents

Let's Get Better Acquainted 1
What Are The ED Principles? 5
The Subconscious Mind 8
Negative Imprinting 41
The Effects of Negative Imprinting 47
Stress 50
Energy Vampires 54
The Language of Manifestation 65
The Law of Resonance 68
The Law of Vibration 74
The Law of Attraction 83
Forming Positive Expectations 104
Inner World, Outer World 108
An Empowering Environment 114
A Successful Mindset 117
Positive Thinking and Self-Talk 119
Affirmations 125
Afformations 130
Meditation and Relaxation 135

Guided Meditation	143
Visualization	146
Listen To Your Intuition	155
Thought Field Therapy	159
EFT Tapping	162
Meridian Tapping Techniques	164
Ho'oponopono	165
Raise Your Vibration	168
Awaken Your Spirit	170
Live Fearlessly	171
Change Is Necessary For Growth	175
Gratitude	179
Do What You Love	183
The Power of the Mind	198
What Do You Believe?	206
The Zone	211
Happiness	214
Living Your Greatness	216
In Summation	219
Further Acknowledgement	223
Buddhist Prayer of Forgiveness	227
Bibliography	228

Affiliate Links 265
About the Author 325

A journey of a thousand miles begins with a single step.
Lao-tzu (Chinese philosopher 604 to 531 BC)

Let's Get Better Acquainted

A Special Education teacher by profession, long have I been a student of Metaphysics, as my Amazon Author Page will easily attest.

An avid reader, I love to play with words.

I love to orchestrate words.

I love to rearrange words.

I simply love words, even when there are no words to adequately describe what I am feeling (which, often enough, can be the case with the English language).

I simply must write.

Writing is as much an integral part of my BEingness as is breathing.

As both an avid reader and researcher, I am also a lover of knowledge, so I keep myself busy, doing my best to specialize in an area that exudes who I am.

Living The ED Principles

One dear friend has told me that I simply *must* keep writing, both printed and Kindle books, because I change lives; as a result, he finds himself *changing daily* because of my books. He tells me that reading my books *always brings positive vibes* to his day.

Another friend has shared that, when reading my books, she *knows* who she is meant to be, she *knows* that the more she reads of my material, the more she *feels the healing beginning*. It is her intent to keep healing and growing.

Another friend recently told me that *every message contains the energy of the writer* and that my words are *potent* (which he meant as a compliment); he loves reading everything that I write because *the words are always so uplifting*. He also tells me that I have *amazing* energy.

I am very much inspired by their words; so, too, am I humbled.

With a fundamental need to grow, Abraham Maslow, an American psychologist, referred to this as self-actualization. In essence, then, life is all about growth.

Living The ED Principles

In the words of Abraham Maslow: *Musicians must make music, artists must paint, poets must write if they are to be ultimately at peace with themselves. What human beings can be, they must be. They must be true to their own nature. This need* [that] *we may call self-actualization refers to man's desire for self-fulfillment, namely to the tendency for him to become actually in what he is potentially: to become everything one is capable of becoming.*[1]

Writing is a gift that I strive to use to the best of my ability. Knowing who I am, I continue to write from my soul. My purpose in writing is to communicate the joy I experience in living.

If my words, courtesy of my writing, can help another, then I am continuing to succeed in both my purpose as well as my passion.

---

[1] http://toolstolife.com/articles/Abraham-Maslow-s-Self-Actualizer-380

Living The ED Principles

With the title for this book coming to me like a flash out of the blue, the rest of the work continued to flow in much the same matter (which is generally the case when I am reading, researching and writing).

I trust that reading <u>Living the ED Principles</u> will serve to inspire you in some way as you venture forth on your own spiritual journey.

As you strive to liberate your life, do remember to be kind to others, yourself included, in thought, word and deed.

What Are The ED Principles?

The ED Principles are comprised of two key components; namely, [1] I <u>expect</u> the best, and [2] I <u>deserve</u> the best.

The word expect can be defined as *looking forward to something that you are regarding as likely to happen*; in essence, you are anticipating its occurrence.

The word deserve, in this example, can be defined as *staking a claim in that which you are expecting*.

It also needs to be shared that belief is associated with the second component.

Many people believe that one should expect the best while also preparing for the worst; why would you want to prepare yourself for something disastrous?

That just seems to negate the expectation, does it not?

Unfortunately, a great many people expect the worst, mainly in an effort to avoid being disappointed.

Living The ED Principles

When you expect the worst, so, too, are you focused on the worst.

Apply this to the Law of Attraction and you merely attract more negativity into your life.

A more positive and effective strategy is to expect the best, building upon that expectation with preparation and action.

Apply this to the Law of Attraction and you will be quite successful in attracting more positivity into your life.

Author Eileen Caddy shares these words …… *Set your sights high, the higher the better. Expect the most wonderful things to happen, not in the future but right now. Realize that nothing is too good. Allow absolutely nothing to hamper you or hold you up in any way.*

As Ralph Marston writes, "Expect the best, and visualize, in great detail, your own participation in it. That puts you into a powerful frame of mind, orients you toward success, and brings your expectations to life. Expect the best, and you enable yourself to recognize and make full use of the opportunities coming your way. Expect the best, while preparing to handle whatever may come along, and you'll be ahead of the game from the very beginning." [2]

While life may not always live up to your highest expectations, when the disappointments do come, having chosen to expect the best eventual outcome means that, more often than not, you will experience the best (that you were able to imagine) for the particular situation.

As Somerset Maugham writes ... *It is a funny thing about life; if you refuse to accept anything but the best, you very often get it!*

In addition, Mark 9:23 reads ... *If thou canst believe, all things are possible to him that believeth.*

---

[2] http://greatday.com/motivate/960927.html

The Subconscious Mind

The subconscious mind is very powerful; in truth, it is unlimited in potential. Once you [1] begin to understand the power of the mind, and [2] learn the laws of the universe, you [3] can reprogram your subconscious so you [4] can live life to the fullest.

There are two things that separate the so-called average person from the successful individual; namely, [1] the choices being made, and [2] the beliefs they were programmed with.

Understandably, the programming that is received from birth, to the present, shapes who you are and what you do. In fact, it is your belief system (programming)that sets you apart from other people.

Every individual on this planet has a belief system that guides their thinking, their reasoning and their actions.

Living The ED Principles

Are you aware of the specific patterns of behavior that allow you to attract into your life that which you desire?

Are you aware of the specific patterns of behavior that serve to repel what you want?

Do you know how to make the shift, from one pattern of behavior to the other, so that you can move from repelling to attracting what it is that you wish to have in your life?

Every action begins with a thought.

The conscious mind (your current state of awareness) takes in what you perceive via the five physical senses (images, sounds, tastes, smells, tactile experiences).

The subconscious mind, then, processes these impressions, sending them back to your conscious mind, in the form of feedback (that also directs and orchestrates your emotions) that you perceive as thoughts.

When these thoughts arise in your conscious mind, they may, or may not, be in harmony with the programming that has been ingrained into you since the day of your birth.

The subconscious mind operates much like the hard drive of a computer. Our operating system, if you will, this is where filed information (memories, habits, programmed beliefs, personality traits) is stored.

By way of example, everyone has a bad experience at some point in their life. The conscious mind inputs that information, sending it to the subconscious for additional processing; the bad experience is then stored, and filed, for later recall.

When faced with a similar experience, albeit at a later date, the subconscious automatically retrieves the memory, which usually results in the individual feeling the same sensation(s) as before.

In truth, the process is quite an ingenious one.

My research has uncovered a non-physical barrier that exists between your conscious and subconscious; a barrier that prevents anything that is in disagreement (with your previous programming)from reaching your subconscious mind.

Dr. Robert Anthony has a name for this non-physical barrier; namely, the *Critical Factor*. He further shares that it is this non-physical barrier that takes what the conscious mind is thinking and then seeks approval from the subconscious mind, in order to pass the information along. Sometimes the subconscious mind allows it to be delivered and sometimes it does not. [3]

Everyone has the ability to have, to do, to be, whatever they want *if they satisfy* all of the conditions that allow them to utilize their competent (and extremely powerful) mind in the manner in which it was intended to be used.

[1] First of all, you must become aware of what you want.

---

[3] Email received November 15, 2013.

[2] Next, you must possess the desire to attain that which you want.

[3] Lastly, you must work on reprogramming your beliefs.

Subconscious reprogramming becomes the mechanism through which old thought processes can be replaced and enhanced.

There are three types of programming that you find yourself contending with throughout your daily life; namely,

[1] Genetic programming: how your body functions, the development of your personality, the talents you develop.

In accordance with genetic programming, researchers have discovered that levels of a molecule called neuropeptide Y (NPY) directly relate to attitudes toward life, meaning that one can either see the glass as half-empty or half-full. [4]

4

http://www.telegraph.co.uk/health/healthnews/8308883/Bor

In keeping with this study, it was discovered that those with lower levels of NPY are much more negative; they find it more difficult to deal with stressful situations and are more susceptible to depression.

It had long been assumed that the reason why we behave the way we do was due to our inherited genetic programming; however, it was recently discovered that we are not prisoners to our genes in that we *can modify our behavior* with our beliefs, and perceptions, by changing our genetic behavior. [5]

[2] Environmental programming: what you learn (as you grow up) from your parents, from the media, from movies, from your peers, from your teachers, from what you read and are told.

Just as parents have an effect on their children, so, too, do children have an effect on their parents; in addition,

---

n-miserable-some-people-genetically-programmed-to-be-negative.html
[5] http://www.happinessgenes.com/changing-our-genetic-behavior-with-epigenetics/another-category/

environmental programming has a direct effect on mental health.

[3] Mass Mind programming (the collective consciousness): programming that you simply absorb without knowing it, such as the beliefs and attitudes that reflect family, country, culture, ethnic background and socio-economic status.

The difficulty then, as stated earlier, lies in getting past the conscious mind in order to directly enter the subconscious and install new programs.

We know that we are creators. We know that we create our reality experience(s) based on the blueprint that exists within our subconscious mind.

We also know that it is possible to change this blueprint, courtesy of subconscious reprogramming.

We know that it is possible to align both the conscious mind and the subconscious mind so that they are in agreement with each other, so that they can work together.

We also know that when this happens, infinite possibility abounds.

Having conscious awareness of some extreme event that literally changes your thoughts and attitudes is one way of reprogramming your mind. By way of example, think about someone you know who has been diagnosed with a serious illness; through a miraculous event, they have suddenly been cured of the disease.

Another way to reprogram your mind is through repetition and reinforcement.

Not simply a matter of saying a word, phrase, or mantra, over and over again, you must engage in some technique that will break the barrier (that prevents certain thoughts from gaining entry into the subconscious area); a technique that, after becoming so ingrained, becomes second nature, mainly because the repetition has entered your subconscious mind and is working from that level.

Living The ED Principles

Dr. Robert Anthony, published author, international personal development trainer, consultant and master hypnotist, has a program called <u>Deliberate Creation Instant Self-Hypnosis</u> [6] wherein he discusses the principle of one brain and two phases of mind power, meaning the conscious and the subconscious; as has already been alluded to, each has different functions, abilities and capacities.

When we talk about the conscious mind, we are talking about one's everyday normal state of awareness; an awareness, albeit limited, that allows one to appreciate the good things in life. Both reason and logic rest in the conscious mind; so, too, are these valuable skills.

In addressing the subconscious mind, this is where we connect with higher (infinite, limitless) intelligence; so, too, is this the area where wisdom, insight, intuition, memories, learning and experience (happy as well as unpleasant) is stored.

---

[6] http://hop.clickbank.net/?chebogue/tsdc1129&x=6minaudio

Living The ED Principles

Unless one is able to change their subconscious blueprint (automatic programming), they will keep getting the same results, no matter how hard they try to change.

The subconscious mind does not normally change immediately; just as it took time for your subconscious blueprint to be created, so, too, will it take time for the blueprint to be changed.

To paraphrase the words of Dr. Robert Anthony, we already exist in a trance state (of happiness, of struggle, of abundance, of poverty).

Courtesy of the <u>Deliberate Creation Instant Self-Hypnosis</u> program, he assists people in dehypnotizing themselves from habits and beliefs that are not getting them what they want.

By going to the subconscious, locating the problem and resolving it, you create true freedom and the ability to live life on your terms.

One of the fastest ways to create subconscious change is through hypnosis.

When you use self-hypnosis, you are able to talk directly to your subconscious mind without any interference.

Once your subconscious knows what you want, you will be guided to the right people, places, circumstances and opportunities that are in alignment with your desire.

You will also learn to take inspired action to make things happen.

The process of reprogramming always seems intimidating at first, primarily because changing long-held beliefs can be a fearful process; many people would prefer to hold onto what is familiar, even if riddled with negativity, rather than risk taking that giant leap of faith into the abyss of the unknown.

You are the one who has to decide to change.

Living The ED Principles

No one else can make that decision for you.

Essentially, it really depends on how badly you want to change.

Once you are ready to take the plunge, thereby embracing what constitutes a life-long process, the first step involves changing your current mindset.

Your subconscious *always* follows your thoughts (and inner beliefs) because they are the very instructions that serve to create situations (in your outer world) that reflect back to you what you think and believe.

The purpose, then, of your subconscious mind is to create what you think (and believe).

Living The ED Principles

You are not giving your subconscious mind the appropriate set of instructions if [1] you are not getting what you want out of life, [2] you are not enjoying the successes that you want, [3] you are not experiencing the happiness that you want, and [4] you find yourself struggling to make ends meet.

Negative thoughts (and beliefs) always block you from succeeding in having the life you want. You, alone, have the power to create the kind of life you want, one based in either positivity or negativity, through the redirection of your subconscious mind.

Most of us have never been taught how to direct (or redirect, if you will) our subconscious mind.

Even more shocking is the fact that most of us have long been directing our subconscious mind, albeit unknowingly, to bring us more of what we do not want.

This is why we struggle.

Living The ED Principles

This is why things never seem to work out.

This is why we seem to experience failure after failure.

This is why we never seem to be able to get ahead.

We exude *dominant thoughts and beliefs* which are the very *instructions that are followed by our subconscious mind*.

What we routinely think about (and strongly believe, of course) is what we get, mainly because this is what our subconscious *thinks* we want.

Your subconscious creates conditions and circumstances based on [1] what you believe, [2] what you feel, [3] how you view life and [4] what you consider to be the truth about your life (and the world at large), primarily because these are your predominant thought patterns.

Living The ED Principles

Even when you truly want that particular job, for example, as long as you believe you cannot attain it, you will never succeed; in many ways, you end up sabotaging your chances, courtesy of negating thoughts and beliefs.

Negative thoughts always prevent you from achieving what you want.

Negative thoughts, combined with strong (and limiting) beliefs, merely lead to failure after failure after failure.

Creating thoughts that empower you, creating thoughts that allow you to succeed, are what enable you to enjoy life.

Your subconscious mind is *far more powerful* than your conscious mind.

Your subconscious mind, then, can be your great partner (and your ally) in achieving success, when you give it the right set of instructions.

Living The ED Principles

By affirming *my subconscious mind is my partner in success*, you are acknowledging that the conscious mind and the subconscious mind can work together.

As stated earlier, the subconscious mind serves to attract conditions and circumstances according to your predominant thought patterns.

It is important, as well, to understand that your subconscious mind is not limited in any way, meaning that it will always attract, to you, according to your thoughts; it merely serves to act upon what resides (and vibrates) within.

Further to this, your subconscious mind will act upon any request, or instruction, you give it.

Any thought that is repeated over and over again will create an imprint within the subconscious; hence, repetition is one of the best ways to program the subconscious mind.

Living The ED Principles

The subconscious mind is unable to distinguish between what is real and what is imagined, what is true and what is false; this is why the usage of visualization, affirmations, mantras and repeated images can have such a powerful effect.

An affirmation is any statement that you affirm, or speak.

A mantra is an affirmation (or phrase) that is repeated over and over.

You can either program yourself for happiness and success or let everything outside of you (meaning media and society) program your mind with fear and thoughts of failure.

It is essential that you understand that thoughts become things; ultimately, the choice lies with you.

This means that just as you can deprogram negative subconscious thoughts, so, too, can you install new positive programs.

Living The ED Principles

Knowing that every thought (and belief) that gains entrance to the subconscious will eventually manifest, you learn to become more diligent in monitoring and directing your thoughts.

In learning how to reprogram your subconscious mind, you learn to [1] control your behavior, [2] break bad habits, and [3] get rid of unwanted (and often unnecessary) emotion.

The subconscious mind learns by repetition; it does not learn by logic.

Your subconscious prefers to talk to you without words (the domain of your conscious and logical mind), meaning through images, music and sounds.

As you learn to tap into your creative side, you are helping your subconscious express itself.

Nurturing your artistic expression (through such mediums as painting, drawing, cooking, decorating, sculpting, pottery, photography, writing, singing and dancing) can help you come to live more authentically, and in closer contact, with your subconscious self.

Hypnosis is one method that can be used to reprogram the subconscious mind.

Far from being asleep or unaware, hypnosis is a wakeful state where you are deeply relaxed and yet have a heightened level of suggestibility as well as a focused awareness.

Hypnosis works by relaxing you into that beneficial Alpha state where your brain shifts its activity; in fact, a brain scan of a person in hypnosis shows the brainwave activity that we experience in the early years of our lives, when our minds were able to soak up information (like a sponge) and immediately integrate it.

This same accelerated learning occurs in hypnosis, bypassing your conscious mind so that your unconscious beliefs and perspectives change quickly and naturally.

Living The ED Principles

The hypnotist uses subtle hypnotic commands to put you into a mild trance, a state where your conscious mind is largely in-active and direct access to your subconscious mind can be gained.

In keeping, positive suggestions can be planted so that changes can be made to long-held belief systems.

Yet another medium that can be used to reprogram the subconscious mind is subliminal messaging.

Subliminal messages are used to shape your subconscious mind in order to align your subconscious thoughts to your conscious wishes and physical actions.

Many people take physical action towards their goals, trying to manifest (whatever it is that they wish) using their mind with practices such as affirmations and vision boards; in many cases, they continue to struggle to see results, either due to [1] deeper held subconscious doubts or [2] lacking beliefs in their ability to manifest.

Most of us are unaware of these deeper subconscious doubts; as a result, subliminal messages can be quite effective.

Tapping directly into your subconscious mind, they serve to eliminate these doubts and negative thoughts so that [1] you are taking action towards your manifestation goals, [2] you are consciously manifesting, and [3] your subconscious mind is completely supportive and positively aligned with your manifestation desires.

Both hypnosis and subliminal messaging are methods of gaining access to your subconscious mind. As well, both bypass your critical thinking function (logical reasoning) in order to reprogram negative behavior.

Albert Einstein discovered that when he listened to music by Mozart, both his analytical prowess and creativity were enhanced.

We now know that Mozart created music that has an effect very similar to modern binaural enhanced learning technology.

Today, we refer to this as Brainwave Entrainment.

Heinrich Wilhelm Dove, a Prussian physicist and meteorologist, discovered, in 1839, that slightly different frequencies, heard simultaneously, would cause the brain to produce a slightly different frequency (tone) that sounded like a beat.

Today, this is what we cite as binaural beats technology. [7]

In 1973, Dr Gerald Oster, a biophysicist, presented a paper in the *Scientific American* that sparked further research and interest into the binaural beats phenomenon; this paper, entitled "Auditory Beats in the Brain," documented how the brain interprets frequency signals and produces the binaural

---

[7] http://www.binauralbeatsmeditation.com/free-mp3/

beat effect, further suggesting the possibilities of hormonally induced physiological behavior changes. [8]

As each of us is perfectly aware, when we hear sounds, the brain responds with a feeling, an emotion, a state of mind, if you will.

As we grow up listening to music, we are influenced by the sound of the music, meaning that different types of music induce different feelings. Our bodies (how we breathe, how we move) are affected by the music that we hear.

Mozart knew this; so did the Beatles, my all-time fab four. As your mind entrains with the binaural beats, your body entrains with the music.

Brainwave entrainment tones induce brainwave patterns that allow you to reach a particular state.

---

[8] http://cherigustafson107.vpweb.com/G%20Oster%20-%20Auditory%20Beats%20in%20the%20Brain.pdf

Brainwave entrainment is any methodology or practice that causes brainwave patterns to slow down, thereby resulting in an altered state of consciousness.

The documented benefits to brainwave entrainment include [1] heightened intuition and psychic power, [2] balancing of both hemispheres of the brain, [3] increased creativity, [4] increased focus, [5] healing of the body, [6] easier to reach a deep (relaxed) meditative state, [7] reduction of stress and anxiety and [8] an induction of calmness.

While the brain does not constitute what we refer to as the mind, the subconscious mind does use the brain to carry out necessary and required functions; a most fascinating marriage of sorts, wouldn't you say?

It also needs to be stated that one's intuitive, or psychic, powers arise from within their subconscious mind.

If you want to focus on getting something, you start the process by thinking about what you want.

This thought, then, proceeds through to your subconscious mind, which, in turn, will act upon said thought.

If this thought is in vibration with the energy of the universe, the end result will be that you will have obtained that which you thought about.

This means that your subconscious programming *must be* in line with what you desire.

If this programming is not in alignment, you will not be in vibration, which, in turn, will serve to deliver more of what you do not want.

Both the Law of Vibration and the Law of Attraction work together with the subconscious mind so that you may live an abundant and prosperous life.

To obtain what you want in life, you must make sure your pre-programmed subconscious mind is in alignment with the vibrations of the universe.

Living The ED Principles

When you develop a thought, it is analyzed by the conscious mind, after which it begins to send out electro-chemicals that travel through the brain, opening neural pathways so that data can be passed along.

During this process, additional cells throughout the brain are imprinted with the data that is being processed.

The conscious mind, then, attaches emotion to the thought, based on its perceived interpretation of the data.

Emotion is what increases the vibration of the thought; your thoughts also serve to establish beliefs that become stored in the subconscious mind.

Interestingly enough, this belief can be based on truth; so, too, can it be based on a complete falsehood. It merely depends on where the thought came from and how it was interpreted (through your lens of bias).

When the conscious mind receives a similar input at some point in the future, the subconscious mind first locates the data that was stored and then sends it back to the conscious

Living The ED Principles

mind with an attached emotion (that was also stored and kept on file).

The frequency of the retrieved data is what creates the vibration.

If this previously stored data matches the vibration of the universe, there is an alignment and the result is the creation (manifestation) of that which the initial thought was intended to provide.

Once again, you need to remember that the subconscious mind does not know the difference between what is real or what is imagined.

If you want to succeed at subconscious programming, you must tend carefully to the garden of your thoughts.

Thoughts direct action.

Thoughts have power.

Living The ED Principles

The secret to success lies in the way that you choose to program your mind.

We all have a tendency to function based on our core beliefs (programming). A great many also commit self-sabotage, simply because they only look at things from the conscious level, meaning that what they see (and hear) is what they believe.

Everything we absorb in our everyday existence affects us both consciously, as well as subconsciously, because what gets fed into our conscious thereafter proceeds to our subconscious.

The life you have right now, the way you act right now, the attitudes and beliefs you have right now, the mindset you hold right now, the paradigm to which you aspire right now, is the way you were programmed from the past; this is why it is vital that you learn to monitor your thoughts as you progress throughout each day.

Living The ED Principles

If you continue to feed negative thoughts into your conscious mind, these thoughts will be processed in your subconscious mind, remaining there for use at a later time.

If you feed your conscious mind uplifting, empowering, positive thoughts, these will also get processed in the subconscious mind, remaining within the stored memory bank for future use.

The subconscious mind does not know what is right or what is wrong; it only processes what it receives. This is why it becomes imperative that you learn to be in control of what the subconscious mind processes.

It is through vigilance that you are able to prevent negative, and disempowering, thoughts from getting into your mind, thereby causing you pain, grief and frustration at a later date.

In order to become the person that you want to be, the person that you deserve to be, the person you intuitively know yourself to be, despite previous programming, you will come to find that you may have to completely alter your core beliefs, replacing them with more constructive and effective beliefs.

The best way to overcome outdated programming is to replace it with new programming.

This is a process that takes time, patience and perseverance.

Just as with computers, subconscious programs can be changed; upgrading one's operating system (to become more functional, to become more secure) is always the best choice.

As you work to download the new program into your conscious (which will be directly fed into the subconscious, and processed accordingly, while also being held in memory for future use), immediate results will be perceivable.

By changing your programming, you can literally change your life.

Living The ED Principles

As you can see, the more you learn about the human mind, as has been evidenced in this chapter, the more you can use this knowledge to enhance your life.

The subconscious will not discriminate.

The subconscious mind will not judge.

The subconscious mind will not censor.

The subconscious mind will manifest success, abundance and health just as easily as failure, dis-ease and misfortune.

Once you have been able to grasp the fact that your subconscious manifests the dominant thoughts and images, it seems as if fortuitous events begin to happen.

This does *not* happen by chance.

As you consciously and deliberately continue to work with your subconscious mind, the people and circumstances you require, to achieve your goals, are drawn to you; this is called synchronicity.

Living The ED Principles

While synchronicity appears to be coincidence or luck, it is neither.

Synchronicity arises, given the natural laws that you have set in motion, with your thoughts.

Modern physics see the universe as a vast, inseparable web of dynamic activity.

Not only is the universe alive and changing, on a constant basis, as are we, but everything in the universe affects everything else; we are all interconnected.

Everything in the universe is made up of energy.

Your thoughts, then, consist of the same energetic substance as the building blocks of the universe.

Living The ED Principles

With your thoughts being energy, it only makes sense that repeated images, affirmations, visualizations, deeply held beliefs, fears and desires, all vibrate within this larger web of dynamic activity, thereby creating your reality experience.

You need to *see* yourself enjoying the freedom of living your life without the dysfunctional beliefs and behaviours that have long held you back.

You also need to *feel* yourself enjoying the freedom of living your life without the dysfunctional beliefs and behaviours that have long held you back.

When you have been able to transform your negative outlook into a positive one, you can begin to achieve that which you have set your mind to accomplishing.

Negative Imprinting

For many years, too numerous to count, like a great many others, I found myself feeling stuck in negative thought patterns. As a result, I always seemed to expect the worst.

Many conversations began with *I don't think that I can* or *I seriously doubt that I can*.

There are so many vocabulary based words that are negative in nature; words like abysmal, annoying, appalling, bad, belligerent, beneath, callous, can't, clumsy, deplorable, depressed, disease, disgusting, dishonorable, dismal, don't, enraged, fail, faulty, fear, feeble, greed, grim, grotesque, gruesome, guilty, hate, hideous, homely, horrendous, imperfect, impossible, insane, jealous, malicious, mean, misshapen, monstrous, negate, never, no, nonsense, not, offensive, old, quit, reject, repulsive, revenge, ruthless, shoddy, shouldn't, sickening, sinister, spiteful, stupid, unable, useless, vicious, vile, vindictive and wary.

Unfortunately, this is the predominantly common mindset that society has foisted upon us, referred to as negative imprinting.

As children, we are constantly bombarded with new ideas, thoughts and words, be it through [1] the beliefs that our parents hold as true, [2] the sayings that our parents (teachers, relatives, friends) impart on a fairly continuous basis, [3] watching television, [4] listening to the radio, and [5] singing the lyrics to popular songs.

Hearing the same message over and over, or even one time if delivered in a strong emotional way, is what serves to create an imprint.

You can easily check for negative imprinting, based on the physiological response of the body, to comments such as

° If you can't get it right, don't do it at all.

° It is only in your imagination.

Living The ED Principles

° Keep your opinions to yourself.

° Money is the root of all evil.

° Money doesn't grow on trees.

° You must think that I'm made of money.

° You have to work hard to earn a decent living.

° You have to give up time with your family to make money.

° I can never seem to get ahead.

° You can't have your cake and eat it too.

° You never do anything right.

° You never should have been born.

° You will never amount to anything.

° You have to learn to make do with what you've got.

° Make sure you eat everything on your plate because there are children in the world who are starving.

° The only person you can count on is yourself.

° There's never enough.

° Just who do you think you are?

° That's not being very realistic.

° Rich people are evil, pompous, arrogant and dishonest (meaning that in order to get rich, you have to be just like them).

° Poor people are mainly nice people whose only goal in life is to make a living for their family and die penniless.

° It is a spiritual aspect of oneself to be in a poor state (because this way you stay humble and worship God without restrictions).

Imprints, then, are subconscious beliefs that we hold as being true.

In essence, negative imprints are beliefs that hold us back from reaching our goals and achieving our dreams and desires.

Stored in our subconscious, they remain with us until they are purified or resolved. Hypnosis, NLP and EFT are excellent tools that can be used; bypassing the conscious mind is what allows for change to take place.

At the same time that a limiting, negative imprint is removed, a positive imprint, that supports the change you want, needs to be installed in its place.

By themselves, positive thinking and affirmations are not enough to change a belief mindset and thought pattern; one has to truly feel, believe and own the emotions that these affirmations generate.

As we know, every word we utter carries a vibrational frequency.

Living The ED Principles

When you repeat certain words, it becomes through the feeling, believing and owning the associated emotions that you are, in effect, changing your own vibrational frequency.

So, too, must this new vibrational frequency be married with inspired action to further support the new truth, the new belief, the new attitude towards life.

The formula is simple ……

words + feelings + actions = result (outcome)

Affirmations work best just before you arise in the morning (while you are still in the Alpha state) or just before you fall asleep at night (while you are beginning to enter the Alpha state).

Stated while conscious (or in a very light trance), your subconscious mind requires constant repetition, before adopting the new imprint or habit.

The Effects of Negative Imprinting

An energy imprint translates as being residual energy that remains in place after the source of that energy (person or incident) is no longer in place (or has ceased to exist).

The stronger the emotional charge, the more powerful the energy imprint. People with strong empathic abilities can detect these more readily than others, but many people can train themselves to do so (or be trained by others).

If they are not cleared, negative energy imprints, particularly those carrying a strong charge, will attract more of the same (or similar) energy. For those who are familiar with the Law of Attraction, it is known that like attracts like.

Negative experiences create expectations, thereby setting the tone for future beliefs, values and behaviors. In fact, these highly emotional experiences create life patterns which seem unrelenting and invincible to change. People often feel imprisoned by them, making it difficult to live satisfying lives.

Negative imprints generate a plethora of unsatisfactory behaviors to which we, unfortunately, become accustomed over time; as adults, we continue to engage in these (and similar) behaviors in a variety of situations, because that is all we know.

Several common negative imprints may include

[1] Suspicion or distrust (may have been mistreated, physically, sexually or emotionally, as children)

[2] Emotional Impoverishment (stems from inadequate parental nurturing)

[3] Helplessness

[4] Anxiety

[5] Codependence

Recognizing the various negative imprints in our lives is the first step toward creating healthier, more positive change.

Living The ED Principles

It is important to begin to understand that the main causes of dis-ease are negative thoughts, negative actions and negative imprints.

Everything starts in the mind before manifesting on the physical plane.

So, too, does this mean that we need to tackle the issue at the same level; namely, the level of the mind.

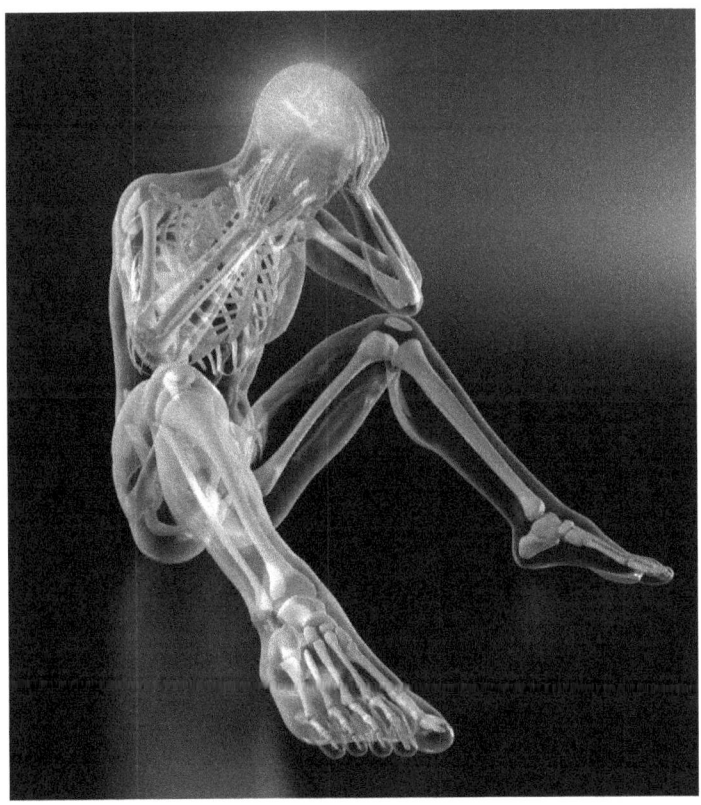

Stress

The human body is designed to [1] experience stress and [2] react to it.

When stress keeps us alert, so as to be ready to avoid danger, this is the positive reaction.

Stress becomes negative when a person facing continuous challenges is unable to experience any relief or relaxation between these difficult situations; when we feel overworked in this way, stress related tension continues to build.

Stress that continues, without relief, can lead to a condition called distress, which, in turn, leads to physical symptoms that may include headaches, upset stomach, heartburn, obesity, a lowered immune system, elevated blood pressure, chest pain and insomnia.

Research also suggests that stress can bring on, or worsen, certain symptoms or diseases.

Stress, then, becomes our own worst enemy.

Living The ED Principles

It also needs to be understood that stress is an *adaptive* response, meaning that with the correct coping mechanisms, we have the ability to retrain our minds to respond (react) differently; this also means that we have the ability to counteract the potential damage(s) that stress can cause.

We know there to be a profound connection between body and mind. That having been said, each of us also has it in our power to [1] reverse the negative effects of stress, and [2] find a positive and beneficial outlet for the stress.

Physical activity helps the mind and body together process stressful situations. The hormones that are released, such as adrenaline and epinephrine, make us feel good.

Practiced for thousands of years, meditation is now enjoying a widespread acceptance amongst both medical practitioners and holistic specialists.

By focusing and centering the mind, the immediate (and often unconscious) reactions caused by stress can be processed in a way that is more productive than the body taking the full impact.

Given that stress can cause feelings of isolation, social interaction can have a major impact on how one handles stress, mainly because [1] one might get the advice they need, [2] one might be guided to see things from a different vantage point, and [3] one might begin to visualize other possibilities, thereby changing their initial perspective.

Another factor not to be overlooked is obtaining the correct amount of sleep, given that [1] sleep helps to heal the body from the physical rigours of day to day life, [2] sleep allows the mind to process information, [3] sleep often gives us the clarity of thought that is needed, and [4] sleep also presents us with a fresh start, from a psychological standpoint, if you will, so that we can begin the following day with the energy that is needed to deal with situations as they present themselves.

Living The ED Principles

Only you have the power to change your thought processes.

Will you continue to suffer needlessly, without change, or will you endeavour to turn the problematic situation into a solution that serves to benefit?

Energy Vampires

Energy Vampire is a term that is used to refer to people, metaphorically speaking, who leave you feeling exhausted, emotionally or mentally depleted, unfocused and depressed.

Psychic Vampire and Psychic Parasitism are other related terms.

One of the most effective protection procedures, known as the Finger Interlock Technique, is easy to implement, and its effects are instant.

To begin this technique, simply bring together the tips of your thumb and middle finger of each hand to form two circles, then bring your hands together to form interlocking circles while envisioning your body enveloped in a bright sphere of impenetrable energy, and finally relax your hands and simply affirm, *I am now energized and fully protected.*[9]

---

[9] http://www.llewellyn.com/journal/article/513

Living The ED Principles

In addition, the Finger Interlock Technique has many other useful applications.

Overcoming stage fight, improving memory, and promoting positive social interactions are all within its scope; so, too, can this technique be used to induce instant relaxation during important examinations, public presentations, and conferences, to list but a few of its many applications. [10]

Samantha Fey, an Intuitive Medium, suggests some of the following protective actions [11] ...

[1] Crossing your arms in a folded position over your chest protects your solar plexus chakra (your seat of personal power).

[2] Use the Mirror Effect to protect yourself in advance by visualizing mirrors surrounding you from head to toe because this will deflect negativity back to the source.

---

[10] http://www.llewellyn.com/journal/article/513
[11] http://www.beliefnet.com/Entertainment/Astrology/Five-Ways-to-Protect-Yourself-From-Energy-Vampires.aspx

One way to do this is to imagine a glittering disco ball in front of you; as you see yourself walking inside this disco ball, know that the little mirror squares are shining out all around you, offering you more than adequate protection.

[3] You can also freeze them out.

Taking a plastic water bottle, you write down the name of the Energy Vampire or Vampires in your life.

After placing this slip of paper in the water bottle, you simply put the water bottle in the freezer, thereby freezing their energy so that it does not affect yours.

[4] The color Pink has a nurturing, calming energy.

When you find yourself around an angry, negative person, close your eyes and imagine wrapping them in pink cotton candy.

As you work to infuse their energy with the loving light of pink, you will see their anger dissipating.

Living The ED Principles

In summation, you cannot change an Energy Vampire; sometimes the best protection from a negative person is simply to walk away.

Remembering that like attracts like, the more you walk your truth, living a spiritual life, the less attracted these people will be to you.

An energy vampire is someone who cannot sustain their own energy (or life force) so they feed off others who are at a higher energetic level; generally unhappy, in their struggle to find the joy within, they often seek it outside of themselves. [12]

Amy describes 9 different energy vampire personality types; namely, [13]

[1] The Victim who feels that the world is against them.

---

[12] http://trueshiningself.com/10-tips-to-protect-yourself-from-energy-vampires/
[13] Ibid.

[2] The Blamer who cannot take responsibility for their own actions.

[3] The Drama Queen who constantly looks for attention.

[4] The Charmer (the talker, the jokester) who wants to be the center of attention.

[5] The Green Eyed Monster who always wants what others have and is never satisfied with what belongs to them.

[6] The Guilt Tripper who uses shame to get what they want.

[7] The Gossiper who looks for drama in the lives of others, mainly because they are not happy with their own life.

[8] The Insecure who pulls others down to their low self esteem level.

[9] The Paranoid Android who, while highly anxious and fearful, causes chaotic imbalances in those around them.

Not normally a conscious endeavor, it is important to understand that these individuals can be a family member, a friend, a colleague, a neighbor, a daily acquaintance (based on the stores, shops and places that you frequent); at times, you, yourself, may also be an energy vampire.

Further to this, Amy also addresses the signs and symptoms of having been in contact with, and attacked by, an energy vampire [14] …

º You feel exhausted, lethargic, tired, weak or sick (even after a telephone conversation)

º You are unfocused

º You feel depressed

º You may have developed a headache

º You notice a clammy (sweaty) feeling when in their presence

º You feel fearful

---

[14] http://trueshiningself.com/10-tips-to-protect-yourself-from-energy-vampires/

Living The ED Principles

° You feel unworthy

° Your chest immediately tightens when you meet them

In accordance with Jennifer O'Neill, there are 5 signs easily affiliated with an energy vampire; namely, [15]

[1] people who are negative

[2] people who are depressed (sad, needy or critical) most of the time

[3] people who are searching to fill a void in their life

[4] people who are Drama queens

[5] people who are angry

---

[15] http://trueshiningself.com/10-tips-to-protect-yourself-from-energy-vampires/

Living The ED Principles

I have just discovered that narcissistic people are also energy vampires.

Kaleah LaRoche talks about how "the perpetrator is not normally aware of how his actions are affecting others; on the contrary, the perpetrator often feels he is the one being victimized." [16]

It is true that in healthy relationships, we feed each other by sharing energy; in this case, however, it is a give and take energy exchange that is mutually beneficial.

Energy vampires only take; they never give.

Kaleah also shares that a psychic vampire or energy vampire is an emotionally and spiritually depleted individual, cut off from the true self within. [17]

By comparison, an emotionally and spiritually healthy individual will plug themselves into the source of life in order to restore himself energetically and spiritually, through

---

[16] http://www.narcissismfree.com/psychic-energy-vampires.php
[17] Ibid.

Living The ED Principles

such means as prayer, meditation, yoga, spending time in nature, spending time in quiet reflection. [18]

Socrates was so right when he spoke of the necessity of *knowing thyself*.

While not an easy thing to do, this maxim reflects the importance of taking the journey within to explore the depths of your own being; the basis for all knowledge, as you come to understand the truth about who you are, so, too, have you the capacity to understand others on a much deeper (and often times, esoteric) level.

The term life force energy has many names: ka, chi, ki, prana, tachyon energy, bioplasmic energy, and orgone, to name but a few. [19]

---

[18] http://www.narcissismfree.com/psychic-energy-vampires.php

Living The ED Principles

When we are connected to the Source, we feel truly alive; one of the reasons why spiritual retreat is necessary for the restoration of the human spirit. [20]

Unfortunately, when we allow ourselves to be controlled on some level, be it through fear, anger, pain, rejection, a desire to please, or the need for approval, we give our energy away. [21]

By focusing our energy on the person we are angry at, we give a large portion of our energy away to them.

When we feel humiliated (rejected or hurt) by a relationship, we also tend to give our energy to that person, courtesy of our constant obsession on them and the "what ifs" of the past situation that cannot be changed and/or undone.

In abuse relationships, we readily surrender our energy and power in order to avoid conflict and/or further abuse.

---

[19] http://www.higherawareness.com/manifesting-abundance/life-force-energy.html
[20] http://www.narcissismfree.com/psychic-energy-vampires.php
[21] Ibid.

Whenever we suppress our voice (meaning our energy and our personal power), we are presenting it to the other person on a silver platter, so to speak.

Having experienced this, first hand, in my place of work, I know, full well, that the only way for us to take our energy and power back is to stop giving it away; so, too, do we need to do our best to remove ourselves from disrespectful and abusive environments, which often proves extremely difficult (and sometimes impossible) in the work place.

I knew that I had to take the time to focus on myself, doing everything that could be done to restore my health, and empowerment, on all levels: mental, emotional, physical and spiritual.

As a Crystal Healing Practitioner, unable to change the situation, the best that I could do was to begin carrying specific crystals on my person.

The Language of Manifestation

Manifestation is closely affiliated with quantum physics.

Long has there existed a dance between the physical world and the spiritual world; the manifest and the non-manifest.

Simply observing something changes both the thing being observed as well as the observer is the scientifically proven truth that is the very foundation of quantum physics; a truth that completely contradicts the former mindset that we are inconsequential in the grand scheme of life.

This scientifically proven truth essentially means that *it is the way we observe* (think about, feel about, talk about) *our life that serves to create our reality experience.*

The Law of Attraction appears to focus one's attention outward, into the tangible physical world.

Living The ED Principles

Knowing that everything manifests on the spiritual (unseen) plane first, understanding your connection to Source is paramount; this is where you come to realize that you are actually tapping into a desire that already exists within, be it [1] peace of mind, [2] joy, [3] enthusiasm, [4] achieving a sense of balance, or [5] achieving a sense of enlightenment, for these are the very objectives that reflect the inner truth of your connection to Source.

In our attempts to manifest different conditions in our lives, we are really after these internal states.

Once you have come to the realization that what you are outwardly seeking already exists within you, that wealth and abundance is available the moment you chose to recognize and allow yourself to be fully present to this fact, the realization of your dreams (in the outer world) becomes so much easier because you are already resonating with the vibration of your desire.

Living The ED Principles

What you embrace in your inner world creates what you come to fully experience in your outer reality experience.

I think therefore I am.

I am therefore I have.

Manifestation Steps

1. Focus on the desired outcome with a clear thought.

2. In holding this thought to the forefront of your mind, feel the emotions associated with *already having achieved* this goal; tapping into the expansive emotional experience so that you create the resonance that is needed.

3. Entering into an even deeper state, while concentrating solely on the emotional experience, allows to experience the feeling(s) associated with your desire outcome.

The Law of Resonance

The Law of Resonance holds the key to manifestation.

In keeping, it is the Law of Resonance that serves to provide the answers as to how the Law of Attraction operates.

If an object vibrates at a certain rate of vibration, everything in its vicinity, that has the same vibration, will start vibrating at that same frequency.

In terms of human receptivity, this means that if someone entertains a quality (or problem) that we, to some degree, also entertain ourselves, we will immediately resonate with that person.

This could well be the basis for the saying *birds of a feather flock together*.

Things that vibrate (thoughts, feelings, emotions, ideas, actions, beliefs) at the same frequency create resonance; it is this very resonance that determines what we attract or repel, consciously or otherwise.

All of the events, conditions and circumstances in your life, have been made possible, courtesy of the Law of Resonance.

The Law of Resonance (which also works in harmony with the Law of Attraction) *determines precisely what you will attract into your life based on the resonance* (the frequency or vibration of the energy) *that you are projecting.*

The Law of Attraction merely uses individual resonance (the energy that you are projecting) to produce outcome(s) in the physical realm (tangible manifestations from the spiritual realm).

Living The ED Principles

In short, the Law of Attraction (the delivery system) *engineers precisely what you have asked for,* based on your resonance.

The Law of Resonance simply determines the vibrational intensity of what it is that you are choosing to project.

The emotions that you experience determine the resonance that you project; the emotions that you experience activate, and further enable, the Law of Attraction.

The end result is that you begin attracting, to you, precisely what you are asking for based on the resonance (frequency of energy) that you are projecting.

The job of the Law of Attraction is to attract to you, and bring into your physical existence, what you are asking for as a result of your projected frequency(resonance); this resonance is created, and projected, as a result of the attached emotions.

Living The ED Principles

The Law of Resonance is the law that determines how everything is manifested in your physical world.

Resonance is the outgoing frequency, akin to an outbound radio frequency, that you project.

In continuation, it is the quality of your thoughts (emotions, feelings, ideas and beliefs) that determine the vibrational intensity of the energy you emit (which then determines what is attracted to you).

A frequency of fear and a frequency of love vary significantly in vibrational intensity.

A vibrational output of something feared will only resonate with, and draw to you, a harmonious frequency that produces more of that which is feared. A vibrational output of something loved, or desired, will only resonate with, and draw to you, a harmonious frequency that results in a physical manifestation of that which is loved and desired.

Love emits, and projects, a much higher frequency than does fear; hence, love is far more powerful in attracting to you the things that are loved or desired.

As you can see, it becomes imperative that you learn to become more conscious of your thoughts.

It is also equally important that you experience only the emotions (love versus fear) that are in alignment with what you are choosing to attract, and manifest, on the physical plane.

In summation, everything is connected through vibration.

This is why it becomes important to understand that your thoughts (feelings, attitudes, emotions, ideas, beliefs and actions) also have this resonance, for they can easily be monitored.

In sending forth your vibrations, you become a radio transmitter of sorts for a universal match.

The vibration that is returned to you possesses the exact same characteristics as the energy you have taken the time to broadcast (for all to hear).

The key is this: *when you know how to live in resonance* (meaning the same frequency) *with what you want, synchronicity abounds.*

This is when you know that you have begun to speak the language of manifestation (the language of the universe).

Whilst it is unknown to whom the following words belong, there is much truth to them.

Everything is energy and that's all there is to it. Match the frequency of the reality you want and you cannot help but get that reality. It can be no other way. This is not philosophy; this is physics.

The Law of Vibration

Just as a pebble creates vibrations that appear as ripples, which travel outward, atop a body of water, so, too, do your thoughts create vibrations that travel outward into the universe.

From a scientific perspective, everything that exists, whether capable of being viewed by the naked eye or not, emits a vibrational resonance.

Everything comes from somewhere or something (a Source); in keeping, we can assume that vibration comes from this same Source (known by many names).

Whether a spirit being or thought consciousness, this Source has been referenced as being omniscient, omnipresent, omnipotent, all knowing, all seeing, the Alpha and the Omega.

Living The ED Principles

The entire universe (ourselves included) exists, in its most basic form, as a vibration.

An integral aspect of this same Source (that some call Universal Consciousness), we are here to live, realize and experience both oneness as well our own unique, and personal, individuality.

Just as a drop of water is a part of, and makes up, the body of water that we refer to as a lake, collectively, all of us make up the whole.

We know that atoms are the basic building blocks of matter.

We know that atoms join together to form molecules, which, in turn, form most of the objects present in our physical lives.

We know that atoms are composed of particles called protons, electrons and neutrons.

Protons carry a positive charge, electrons carry a negative charge, and neutrons carry no charge at all.

We know that protons and neutrons cluster together in the central part of the atom, called the nucleus.

We know that electrons orbit the nucleus, creating a vibratory pattern.

On July 4, 2012, it was announced that a new subatomic particle, looking very much like the Higgs Boson (aka the God Particle), [22] had been discovered.

Everything that exists, both seen as well as unseen, consists of a rate of vibration.

Thoughts are vibrations.

Words are vibrations.

Sounds are vibrations.

Light is a vibration.

22

http://www.theatlantic.com/technology/archive/2012/07/still-confused-about-the-higgs-boson-read-this/259472/

Colors emit a vibration.

Our planet is a vibration.

Our entire universe, and everything within it, is a vibrating mass of atoms and subatomic particles.

This means that what we see in our physical lives is not solid; instead, everything is a vibrating mass of energy that merely looks to be solid.

What you are vibrating, you attract.

In the beginning stage of the Law of Attraction, this is what can be referenced as your thought(s).

In the intermediate stage of the Law of Attraction, this is what we refer to as your feeling(s).

In the fully developed stage of the Law of Attraction, this is what is known as your will (or intention).

Living The ED Principles

The more attention you pay to something, the more attention it pays to you.

It is imperative, therefore, that you learn to become conscious of your choices (what you think, what you feel, what you say, what you do).

You can learn to correct the imbalances that often exist between your current state and your desired state by associating with the energy sources that vibrate with the qualities that you desire.

In learning to master a conscious, deliberate and harmonious vibration (in your day to day existence), you will begin to use the creative power of the Law of Vibration to manifest the abundance and happiness that has always been (and always will be) available to you.

It is my belief that we are here, in physical form, to enjoy life; so, too, are we here so that God/dess can live, all that is possible, through us.

Living The ED Principles

If you choose to become fully aware of the Law of Vibration, learning how to align and harmonize your thoughts, feelings and actions with said law, you will discover how to purposefully, and consciously, attract to you, the life that you have always dreamed of having; a life of joy, a life of fulfillment, a life of inner peace, a life of limitless prosperity.

Since everything in the universe is energy, and all energy carries a vibration, our universe, as stated earlier, is one that is vibrationally based.

That having been said, we are constantly sending out vibrational signals that are either attracting or repelling what we want.

The Law of Vibration states that everything in the universe, no matter what it may be, is energy.

Living The ED Principles

Knowing that energy vibrates at different rates (speeds), when the vibration is within our frequency range, we can hear, or see, the vibrating source of energy.

Given that we are energy in the form of a physical body, so, too, do we vibrate like everything else.

Every part of us is a vibration, including our thoughts, our feelings, our emotions, our actions, our psychological states, meaning that when we are aligned with the universe in vibration, we will be able to attract whatever that vibration points to.

Knowing that our thoughts must vibrate in alignment with the universe for us to achieve what we wish, we need to monitor our thoughts (within our conscious mind as well as our subconscious mind) to ensure that all input, and output, is in vibration (harmony) with the universe.

Living The ED Principles

The Law of Attraction is a universal law that enables us to experience the fact that that there is a cause and effect to everything we think, do (or not do) and say.

If we continue to think a particular thought, positive or negative, we simply end up attracting that very thought to ourselves, wanted or not.

It is your vibrational self that attracts compatible patterns.

If you want to experience something different in your life, you have to change the signals that you are sending out.

If you want to attract what it is that you desire, you must learn to set up an attraction for it.

To do this, you need to ensure that the thoughts within your subconscious mind are geared toward what it is that you are trying to attract; otherwise, the subconscious will serve only to attract more of what you do not want.

As a universal law, the Law of Attraction never goes away.

Living The ED Principles

To some degree, it can be controlled, courtesy of what you vibrate to, based on what it is that your thoughts are geared towards.

The end result is simple.

If you reprogram your subconscious mind to vibrate with the universe, you can achieve that which you set your mind to, simply by thinking it into manifestation.

The Law of Attraction

All things that exist within our universe are composed of energy (or vibration).

The Law of Attraction keeps this energetic vibration flowing effortlessly.

The Law of Attraction has also been referred to as one of *cause and effect.*

The Law of Attraction delivers to all, in exactly the same way, with the same unwavering (and predictable) certainty, no matter your age, gender, sexuality, religious belief or nationality.

The Law of Attraction does not differentiate.

The Law of Attraction does not discriminate.

The Law of Attraction does not judge.

Living The ED Principles

The only control that you, as an individual, have as pertains to the Law of Attraction is the free will choice that you exercise, meaning that what you *give* (courtesy of your vibration) is what you *receive*.

If you wish to consciously create a certain result, you must first learn to consciously align your thoughts, feelings, words, beliefs and emotions with the desired outcome.

Thoughts are a vibration; everything that has been manifested first began with a thought.

The thoughts that we think are the very vibrational frequencies that we broadcast out into the universe; these thoughts, then, attract to them vibrations of the same resonance, which manifest on the physical plane.

Our thoughts become what we see.

Our thoughts become what we experience in our outer world experience.

Living The ED Principles

From a scientific standpoint, our thoughts, then, demonstrate a correlation to the item that has been manifested.

The basics of quantum physics state that everything around you (people and objects that surround you, your physical being, your thoughts and emotions) is made of pure energy.

Energy vibrates, meaning that your thoughts (words, actions, deeds, psychological moods) vibrate at a certain frequency. Everything vibrates at a certain frequency, including sound.

When energy vibrates, it attracts other objects that also vibrate at the matching frequency. This means that when your thoughts are focused and empowered by a strong emotion that matches them, they are attracting things to you.

The Law of Attraction states that......

[1] thought energy is released into the universe

[2] thought energy creates, and emits, a specific vibratory pattern (or frequency)

[3] based on the type of thought(high energy, low energy) the quality of thought (positive resonance, negative resonance) and the consistency of thought, this frequency attracts, and is joined by, like energy of the same vibration (resonance)

[4] this serves to create the events, conditions and circumstances that you see manifest in your life

As a result, you can literally attract, unto yourself, that which you have consistently given thought to.

Creation is yet another world for thought made manifest.

Whatsoever things ye desire when ye pray, <u>believe</u> that you receive them and ye shall have them. Mark 11:24.

Established <u>beliefs</u> *always* begin as a <u>thought</u>.

Living The ED Principles

Established beliefs are *always* attached to, and intensified by, an <u>emotion</u>.

The combination of thought, emotion and belief creates an intensified vibration that outwardly projects a frequency. This frequency attracts additional vibrations of a harmonious nature, and the end result is that which you believe (think about) is made manifest in the physical world.

I tell you the truth, if you have faith as small as a mustard seed, you can say to this mountain, "Move from here to there" and it will move. Nothing will be impossible for you. Matthew 17:20.

Faith, like belief, begins with a thought.

Faith is the substance of things <u>hoped for</u>, the evidence of things <u>not seen</u>. Hebrews 11:1.

The thought develops the belief.

The thought correlates with its object, yet unseen, to make it manifest in the physical world.

As a man thinketh, so is he. Proverbs 23:7.

Whatever your thoughts consist of, they always manifest to create your reality experience.

The moment that you change your thoughts, so, too, do you change your beliefs; the moment that you change your beliefs, so, too, do you change your world.

We are what we think. All that we are arises with our thoughts. With our thoughts, we make our world. Buddha

All that we are is the result of what we have thought. If a man speaks or acts with an evil thought, pain follows him. If a man speaks or acts with a pure thought, happiness follows him, like a shadow that never leaves him. Buddha

Living The ED Principles

All things appear and disappear because of the concurrence of causes and conditions. Nothing ever exists entirely alone; everything is in relation to everything else. Buddha

Three are the dwellings of the sons and daughters of Man. Thought, feeling and body. When the three become one, you will say to this mountain "move" and the mountain will move. The Kabbalah

Now is the time to take stock of your life.

If you want to know what it is that are you thinking, the results you see (events, conditions and circumstances) in your own life are what serve to determine the answer.

Your outside (physical) world is always determined by your inner (spiritual) world or thought process (mental world); this merely means that your outside (physical) world is a direct manifestation of your inner consciousness or thoughts.

As a result, you are fully responsible for that which you create (manifest) in your life.

Life does not happen to you; life is created by you.

There are four levels of consciousness that we, as humans, are capable of.

In BETA, we are in our wakeful, everyday, state.

The ALPHA state, known as a relaxation state, is much akin to that which you experience during meditation.

In THETA, we are in more of a dreaming sleep state and/or a deep meditative state.

The DELTA state is synonymous with a dreamless sleep state (much like a coma type state).

Operating from the lowest energy activity from within the brain is what enables you to remain in a vibrational frequency that continues to attract what is desired.

Living The ED Principles

It is in this state that you are able to consciously utilize the Law of Attraction to attract that which you desire.

The Beatles, in their song *All You Need Is Love*, were clearly onto something. With love being both a high energy and positive frequency, this is an emotion that continues to sustain a strong attraction factor.

What you say creates what you believe.

What you believe impacts how you behave.

What you believe impacts the choices you make.

What you believe impacts the way your life will be.

The power of *intentional language* can change your life,

Phrases such as ……

[1] I love myself.

Living The ED Principles

[2] I approve of myself.

[3] I make the right choices every time.

[4] I trust my intuition to guide me.

[5] What I have to offer this world matters.

[6] I wholeheartedly embrace my uniqueness.

[7] Every situation always works out for my highest good.

[8] Wonderful things unfold before me.

[9] I am excited by all of the good that continues to flow into my life.

[10] I believe that the best is possible.

[11] I can see the good in all things.

[12] I can see the good in myself.

[13] I replace my anger with understanding and compassion.

[14] I accept responsibility if my anger has hurt anyone.

[15] I may not yet understand the good in this situation, but it is there to be discovered.

[16] I choose to find hopeful and optimistic ways to look at this situation.

[17] I ask for help and guidance if I am unable to see a better way.

[18] With each step I take, I allow peace to guide me.

[19] I trust myself to keep making the best and smartest decisions for me.

[20] I engage in work that impacts this world in a positive way.

[21] I believe in my ability to change the world, on a small scale, with the work that I do.

[22] I fill this day with hope, love and optimism, facing it with joy and enthusiasm.

[23] I approve of who I am, knowing full well that I am only getting better.

[24] I embrace the rhythm and flow of my own heart.

[25] I am deeply fulfilled with who I am.

[26] My body is healthy.

[27] My mind is brilliant.

[28] My soul is tranquil.

[29] Happiness is a choice and I choose to base my happiness on both my accomplishments as well as the blessings that I continue to receive.

[30] I live an abundant life.

[31] My future is an ideal projection of what I am envisioning now.

[32] With my efforts being continuously supported by the universe, my dreams manifest into reality before my eyes.

[33] I radiate passion, purpose and prosperity.

[34] I wake up each day with strength of heart and clarity of mind.

[35] I am at peace with all that has happened, is happening, and will happen.

[36] As a spiritual being, my very nature is Divine.

[37] My life is just beginning.

…… are examples of what we refer to as *intentional language* (language used with intent to create positive change); so, too, are they called affirmations.

Taking the time to feel the impact behind these words is what serves to bring about empowering change.

If you have studied the Law of Attraction at all, you know that your thoughts, words, emotions and actions transmit an energetic frequency out to the universe.

What we send out always comes back to us; think of it as the boomerang effect, meaning that whatever is vibrating at your transmitted frequency will automatically be pulled back into your reality experience.

Living The ED Principles

If you emit low vibrations (as in anger, fear, cynicism, disappointment, loneliness, lack, sadness, confusion and stress), so, too, will you attract corresponding people, circumstances, experiences and events.

If you emit high vibrations (like joy, love, excitement, abundance, pride, comfort, confidence and passion), so, too, will you attract corresponding people, circumstances, experiences and events.

As long as your vibrational signal remains unchanged, the results that you attract will continue to remain the same.

In knowing, and believing, that you *expect and deserve the best*, you need to avoid negative talk (complaining, arguing, blaming, engaging in doom and gloom conversations, using words like try, can't, should, could, have to, when and if when engaged in self-talk); you need to avoid anything that contradicts your positive expectations, anything that serves to bring you down.

It may also be necessary to limit the amount of time you spend with negative people; when these people have finally been evicted from your life, you will start living your life as you will it to be.

Taking the time to surround yourself with like-minded souls and uplifting spirits makes it much easier to achieve your dreams.

There is always something to be thankful for.

Starting your day with an attitude of gratitude, an attitude of sincere appreciation, for the things that matter to you is a great way to connect with your inner creative powers.

As often as you can, say thank you.

Take the time to smile when you are conversing with others.

Living The ED Principles

Take the time to see the beauty (positive) in situations and appreciate life for the lessons that come your way to learn, to love, to teach by way of example.

As shared by Vishen Lakhiani, founder and CEO of Mindvalley, *gratitude is the key to happiness. When gratitude is practiced regularly and from the heart, it leads to a richer, fuller and more complete life. It is impossible to bring more abundance into your life if you are feeling ungrateful about what you already have because the thoughts and feelings you emit as you feel ungrateful are negative emotions and they will only attract more of those feelings and events into your life.*

If you want things in your life to get better, you have to keep thinking in the direction (alignment) of your goals.

Taking the time to write your goals down strengthens your belief.

Living The ED Principles

Not only does the real magic come from believing in who you are as a person, it also comes from letting go of the emotional baggage of the past.

The Law of Attraction simply states that in life, we attract those things we focus on and think about often, meaning that *our dominant thoughts always find a way to manifest*; hence, the power of the mind revealed.

However, it also needs to be shared that it is not simply the thought alone, but rather the inspired action(s) that the thought generates that serves to produce the desired results.

If we continue to consciously focus our energy on achieving a desired goal, taking full responsibility for our ups and downs, we are in a position to align ourselves to be in the correct frame of mind to succeed; this is when you are able to experience being in the right place at the right time.

Living The ED Principles

My good friend, Carl Harvey, likes to think of the Law of Attraction as *The Law of AttrACTION* because without taking action on your dream, you are left with nothing but a wish unfulfilled.

With the power of positive thinking having been introduced in William Walker Atkinson's book <u>Thought Vibration or the Law of Attraction in the Thought World</u>, [23] the main theory behind the Law of Attraction is that life energy attracts like energy.

The energy that you and I are constantly radiating, outward, is determined by our emotional state (which is often times an unconscious response to an environmental stimulus); as a result, this energy (vibration) can fluctuate constantly. This life energy is what attracts results to you, be they positive or be they negative.

---

[23] http://archive.org/details/ThoughtVibrationOrTheLawOfAttractionInTheThoughtWorld

It was Joseph Murphy who wrote … *The Law of Attraction attracts to you everything you need, according to the nature of your thoughts. Your environment and financial condition are the perfect reflection of your habitual thinking.*

This means that your outer world is a reflection of your inner thinking.

The Law of Attraction exists; in retrospect, it is a basic principle of life.

Not a complex, esoteric, principle, in its entirety it is rather simple: you attract what you think about. In this regard, then, your thoughts become your reality experience; the only problem, being, that it can be extremely difficult to change your inner thoughts, your long-held beliefs.

This is why you need to become clear about what you *really* want.

Visualization is a great way in which to achieve this clarity.

You need to begin to think more positively, enjoying an attitude of gratitude throughout the entirety of your day.

Hypnosis is but one medium through which you can rewrite your thoughts and beliefs.

Hypnosis Live [24] has created four special sessions (Law of Attraction, Attitude of Gratitude, Visualization Success, Positive Thinking) to assist you with this very task.

Availing of related programs, I have continued to make strides with regards to my inner thoughts.

As well, the Law of Attraction Library [25] is a *phenomenal* place to begin your adventure into the Law of Attraction.

It may well be, as they say ... *the world's largest resource for law of attraction information.*

---

[24] http://www.hypnosislive.com/law-of-attraction-hypnosis-bundle
[25] http://www.thelawofattraction.org/

I just know that I am most impressed with their vast collection of free articles and resources.

Forming Positive Expectations

It is possible to turn a negative thought pattern into a positive one. I know because I have succeeded in doing the same for myself. It does, however, require much patience and persistence.

Pay attention first to how you feel.

If you are feeling positive, upbeat and productive, that is an indicator that you have been thinking positive thoughts.

However, if you notice that you are feeling irritable, pessimistic or stressed, you have probably been focusing more on negative thoughts.

The moment this realization comes to you is the very moment whereby you can immediately challenge and change the negative thoughts.

Living The ED Principles

When you encounter obstacles or problems, and you will, try to view them as opportunities to learn from, to grow from, for these are the very same opportunities that will allow you to strengthen yourself as an individual.

When you change your perception, so, too, does your reality experience change.

If you simply work on shifting the way you look at the experiences of your life, you will naturally start forming more positive expectations.

Keep affirming positive self-talk, as in the case of the specific examples that follow.

[1] I know this is going to work out for the best.

[2] I know I will turn this situation to my advantage somehow.

[3] I expect the best and the best always comes to me.

Living The ED Principles

If you expect yourself to succeed, you will succeed.

If you expect yourself to grow as a person, you will grow.

If you expect yourself to be the best that you can be, in any given situation, you will be the best.

You must believe that you are capable of creating the best or you won't be expecting the best.

If you have low expectations, you will get low fulfillment.

If you have high (positive) expectations for yourself, be sure to watch the positive, good, high impact you will have on your life.

Positive reinforcement produces positive action.

Negative reinforcement produces negative reaction.

Living The ED Principles

Thoughts are things; when motivated by emotion (feeling), they become powerful in that they tend to become the reality of your experience.

When you believe in yourself, you are strongly influenced by those feelings.

Employing positive expectations, at every turn, becomes a self-fulfilling prophecy of the best kind.

You must be convinced that you can attain that which you desire; so, too, must you believe in the results that you want.

Inner World, Outer World

The way you think is what you create in your inner world.

The way you talk and act is what you express in your outer world.

As above, so below is a maxim in Hermetic Philosophy; it has been said that this precept originated in the Vedas (a large body of texts originating in ancient India).

The actual text of this axiom, as translated by Dennis W. Hauck from The Emerald Tablet of Hermes Trismegistus, reads *that which is Below corresponds to that which is Above, and that which is Above corresponds to that which is Below, to accomplish the miracle of the One Thing.* [26]

26

http://en.wikipedia.org/wiki/Hermeticism#.22As_above.2C_so_below.22

This simply means that whatever happens on any level of experienced reality (physical, emotional, or mental) also happens on every other level.

Think of yourself as the microcosm, whereby the macrocosm is the universe.

The microcosm is as the macrocosm and vice versa, for within each, also lies the other.

As you come to understand the microcosm (yourself), so, too, are you better able to begin to understand the macrocosm (the bigger picture in the overall schemata of life).

Life does not get better until one begins to make gradual shifts in their thinking.

Living The ED Principles

When I read positive (inspirational) information that warms my heart and inspires me to take action, I know that this serves to help shift my thinking to a higher vibrational level (which is exactly what is needed).

Taking the time to imagine my life (as I want it to be) means thinking, behaving and envisioning myself *already living* the life that I desire.

You must always remain open to every possibility, never hindering yourself. You must decimate scarcity thoughts from your vocabulary base, for limiting thoughts are like thieves in the night; they come to steal everything worth stealing.

We already know that the subconscious mind responds to three key elements; namely, [1] vivid and detailed imagery (sights, sounds, smells, etc.), [2] strong emotion (either positive or negative, it matters naught) and [3] repetition (the more frequent you repeat the exercise, the better).

Living The ED Principles

This translates to seeing, feeling and hearing the experiences that you want and then repeating the same exercise(s) over and over and over again; interestingly, neuroscience is now proving this to be true.

You must develop the mindset necessary to change your inner world because this is what gets reflected back to you, courtesy of your outer world.

Both meditation and guided visualization are wonderful mediums through which to focus the powers of your creative mind.

It was Napoleon Hill, author of Think and Grow Rich, who said that visualization was the only way to reprogram subconscious beliefs; becoming a master at visualization is definitely a step in the right direction.

Creating change is about doing and being committed.

Living The ED Principles

If you want to improve your life, if you want to achieve your goals, you must first make a solid commitment to change, to improve things.

Nothing will ever improve as long as you are distracted.

A commitment to improve your life involves taking action; you start by focusing on what you need to do to create the changes that you want.

Making a commitment sends a message to your subconscious mind; a message that states *I am ready to change and improve my life.*

You must also decide what kind of change you want.

When you allow yourself to work at your full potential (with mind, body and spirit working together), things happen.

When you are able to keep your mind (thoughts) focused on what it is that you want to achieve, meaning your goals, you will succeed.

Essentially, you are learning how to think and create the life you want.

Learning how to control your mind, thereby sending the right messages to your subconscious mind, is what enables you to create the life you want.

Take a look at what it is that you want to achieve in life; think about those goals.

Pay special attention to the negative thought patterns (beliefs) that continually arise when you think about achieving those goals, for these are what will need to be changed.

An Empowering Environment

It is important to realize that you are being programmed, courtesy of your environment; this involves the media, society, at large, and your family.

The moment you become aware of the environmental factors that are affecting your life, you have become empowered.

What, then, can you do to create an even more empowering environment?

The very moment that I knew changes were needed in my life, I stopped reading newspapers, I stopped watching the news, I stopped listening to news on the radio and I stopped buying news related magazines.

In keeping with television, stop watching anything that breeds violence and cruelty, including anything that smacks of living a disempowering life.

Instead, make the time to watch programs that remind you of the brilliant beauty of nature, the wonders of space and the universe, including the magnificence of the animal kingdom.

Immerse yourself in comedy, taking the time to laugh often.

Being an empath, I also had to steer clear of negative people because their troubles quickly became my troubles; you will find yourself quickly depleted of energy.

Take the time to absorb positive, empowering information.

Living The ED Principles

Spend time with positive people who are enjoying success and abundance in their own lives because they will raise your own vibration when you are in their company.

A Successful Mindset

A mind-set is your predominant state of mind (the things you think about, what you focus on, and what you expect from your daily experiences).

For example, if you think negatively, expect the worst to happen, or feel pessimistic about your options, then that is exactly what you will draw into your life.

On the other hand, if you think positively, expect only the best, and focus on a successful outcome, then this is what you can expect to come into your life.

It is also imperative that you believe in yourself (and your capabilities of succeeding at whatever it is that you want to do) while always putting forth your best effort, even when things seem tough.

The individual who demonstrates a successful mindset also understands the importance of consistency, persistence, tenacity and determination.

Living The ED Principles

The individual who demonstrates a successful mindset [1] goes after what they want, [2] thinks optimistically, [3] is not afraid to ask for help, [4] believes they have what it takes to succeed, [5] is willing to take chances, [6] always does their best, [7] always expects the best, and [8] is willing to keep trying, even in the face of adversity.

Positive Thinking and Self-Talk

Positive thinking means that you approach unpleasantness in a more positive and productive way, by thinking the best is going to happen, not the worst.

Positive thinking often starts with self-talk, that endless stream of unspoken thoughts that run through our head every day.

As you know, these automatic thoughts can be positive or negative.

If the thoughts that run through your head are mostly negative, your outlook on life is one of pessimism.

If your thoughts are mostly positive, you are more likely an optimist; someone who practices positive thinking.

Did you know that there are health benefits associated with positive thinking?

Living The ED Principles

Researchers are continuing to explore the effects of positive thinking and optimism on health.

Health benefits may include [1] increased life span, [2] lower rates of depression, [3] lower levels of distress, [4] greater resistance to the common cold, [5] better psychological and physical well-being, [6] reduced risk of death from cardiovascular disease, and [7] better coping skills during hardships and times of stress.

As yet, it is unclear why people who engage in positive thinking experience these health benefits.

One theory is that having a positive outlook enables you to cope better with stressful situations, which reduces the harmful health effects of stress on your body; another theory is that positive and optimistic people tend to live healthier lifestyles.

In essence, it can be said that practicing positive self-talk will improve your outlook.

Living The ED Principles

When you find yourself sharing both your positive mood as well as your positive experience(s), everyone feels the positive energies.

As well, when your state of mind is an optimistic one, you are better able to handle everyday stress in a more constructive way.

A new discipline (neurocardiology) has emerged that focuses on the nervous system within the heart, showing how the heart and the brain communicate with each other.

Up until now, it has always been thought that the purpose of the brain was to control all of the biological mechanisms of the human body.

New evidence, however, is suggesting that the brain is actually the *object* of control as opposed to being the controller.

Living The ED Principles

Current discoveries are telling us that it is the heart that actually controls the brain, particularly in matters of intuition, creativity, spirituality and other so-called right brain modes of thinking.

Continuing research at the Institute of Heart Math (IHM) has discovered that the heart communicates with the brain in four ways: [1] neurological communication (courtesy of the central nervoussystem), [2] biophysical communication (by way of pulse waves), [3] biochemical communication (via hormones of the body) and [4] energetic communication (through magnetic fields).

This research is telling us that the heart sends instructions, if you will, to the brain through each of these channels.

In responding to these cues from the heart, the brain transforms its state to synchronize with that of the heart.

For example, if the heart were experiencing a negative emotional state, it would send corresponding negative cues to the brain.

The brain, in turn, processes these negative messages and directs the rest of the body to respond in like fashion, with everything about the physical body reflecting the negative emotional state as felt by the heart.

Another significant finding, courtesy of the IHM research, is that coherence may occur between two different people when the magnetic field, generated by one person's heart, synchronizes with that of the other person.

This means that any emotional state can be communicated, and shared, with others, thereby causing a contagious wave (be it positive or be it negative) of shared thoughts and emotions.

We have all experienced the electric vibes we feel when we surround ourselves with positive and upbeat people; so, too, have we felt the draining energies we feel when we surround ourselves with negative and gloomy, depressed people.

Living The ED Principles

If the heart can, indeed, influence the mind, it is possible to create affirming opportunities simply by encouraging positive thoughts and emotions; so, too, does this keep the heart in a positive state.

Affirmations

Affirmations (positive, personal, present tense statements) are an effective way to install positive messages into your subconscious mind, thereby overriding embedded negative thinking.

It is in the repeating of these positive statements that you are able to create new and more empowering beliefs (emotions, feelings, thoughts, attitudes).

It is important to use the present tense in your positive affirmations because the subconscious mind knows only the present; likewise, so, too, are you benefitting from the power of time in the now.

Choose only the affirmations that *feel* right to you.

Living The ED Principles

Using the words *I am* or *I have* make the affirmation more powerful.

You must always make use of the strongest, most positive, words and phrases.

Descriptive words also serve to increase the emotional connection you are making with the end result that you want to manifest.

Repetition of affirmations is necessary. Saying them quietly to yourself is effective, provided you say them multiple times each day while also repeating them with authentic positive feeling and expectation.

It is imperative to note that *affirmations will not work if they are not in alignment with your subconscious beliefs*.

If your subconscious beliefs reflect the exact opposite of what it is that you are affirming, your negative programming will always cancel out the other.

For example, if you are affirming that *I am wealthy* and yet your subconscious beliefs are rooted in needing to work hard to make money because life is a struggle and will always continue to be a struggle, then you will simply continue to struggle because this is your underlying mindset.

Once you have been successful in replacing old, negative and limiting beliefs with positive and empowering ones, perhaps through another means, affirmations will then work for you.

After over twenty years of reconfiguring my own subconscious belief patterns, here are some of my personal favorites.

I am the *master* of my life.

I follow the *perfect wisdom* of my heart.

Everything is working together for my *highest good*.

I find *prosperity in simplicity*.

Living The ED Principles

I am *rich in both consciousness and manifestation.*

I am energetic, *replete with vitality.*

I am *good to my body*, and *my body is good to me.*

I am *relaxed and centered.*

My relationships with others are the *mirrors* that show me myself.

I love being able *to give, to create, to share* and *to uplift* others.

I am meant to do *great* things.

Rich is my *natural state of being.*

I exude *passion, purpose* and *prosperity.*

I am thankful for the *limitless, overflowing source of my continued abundance.*

I am *valued and appreciated* for all that I offer.

Living The ED Principles

I am a *mindful and conscious creator*, connected to the great universal power, with every resource at my command.

I live in an *infinite* (limitless) *universe*.

I have the power to attract whatever I wish into my life because the Law of Attraction works; *positive thoughts attract positive circumstances*.

God/dess wants to live, do, and enjoy things *through* my humanity.

It is a *privilege* to be able to *share my knowledge*.

I love money and money loves me; not only are we good *for* each other, we are also good *to* each other.

Afformations

Afformations (a new system devised by Noah St. John) are an important concept in the power of positive thinking.

As is the case with affirmations, afformations also focus on the positive; the key difference, however, is in asking a positive question rather than affirming a positive statement.

Based on Noah St. John's book The Secret Code of Success, an afformation is *the formulation of a question to empower your mind*.

Rather than just stating something is true (as is the case with an affirmation), an afformation asks *why* it is true.

According to Noah St. John, our minds appreciate questions and are eager to search for answers.

He likens this process to an "automatic search function" in the brain, stating that sometimes it is not the answer(s) but the question(s) that makes the difference.

Living The ED Principles

Knowing how powerful our thoughts can be, we repeat positive statements (affirmations) in an attempt to manifest our goals; many people have been quite successful with this approach.

For those who struggle in convincing their minds to believe these statements, afformations can be used to assist in the reframing of one's thoughts.

When you use an afformation to ask a question, it puts a different spin on things because *asking why causes you to stop, think and be in the moment.*

When asking why you attract love in your life, it might be because you are lovable; this, then, leads to further thoughts along the same line. You come to realize that not only do you deserve a loving partner, but you are also attractive, warm, compassionate; you are ready to share your life with that someone special.

Living The ED Principles

As with affirmations, the first step is to decide on what you want.

Once you have identified your goal, you need to formulate a question that assumes you already have what you want.

º Why am I so happy?

º Why am I so wealthy?

º Why is my life so full of joy?

º Why am I feeling abundantly powerful in my thoughts and actions?

º Why do I love and embrace my life?

º Why am I allowed to be, do and have all that I want in life?

Upon asking yourself these questions, you can see that an answer or solution is immediately sought; likewise, evidence to support the answer is also sought. In essence, *the question becomes the answer.*

Living The ED Principles

In taking notice of the answers that come to you, regarding the question(s) that you have posed, you will find that they tend to be positive. Should these thoughts lead to even more questions and positive thoughts, be sure to keep them going.

In asking yourself questions on a regular basis, you will denote that your mode of thinking changes; accordingly, your actions will also follow suit.

You will attract what you seek based on your thoughts and positive vibrations.

As Noah St. John tells us, the Afformation Method is not necessarily about finding the answers; instead, it is about asking the questions that will help you positively manifest your desires. The point of afformations, then, does not lie in finding the answer, but in asking better questions, more empowering questions.

Living The ED Principles

With afformations, you take conscious control of the questions you ask.

Once you start gathering answers to your empowering questions, your internal beliefs begin to shift in a most powerful way.

This changes what the brain focuses on, which, quite naturally, changes how you think.

When you have been successful in changing how you think, your perspective has changed.

Once your perspective has changed, this brings about further change to your actions.

In changing your actions, you will have changed your life.

Meditation and Relaxation

The brain responds to mindfulness practices (meditation and relaxation), thereby increasing neuro-plasticity, a brain malleability activity that allows you to learn new habits, while also adopting constructive (positive) thoughts.

As we go about our day, our brain functions in Beta wave patterns; these are the states associated with waking consciousness.

In meditation, the mind relaxes, your brain patterns slow down, moving first to Alpha and then to Theta; herein, we are more susceptible to suggestion.

By comparison, deep meditation elicits Delta wave patterns; it becomes in entering this state that you notice a change in the quality of your thinking.

All of a sudden, random thoughts come to mind.

Living The ED Principles

In reality, however, they are not random at all; these are the thoughts of your subconscious mind beginning to assert itself on your consciousness.

Your thoughts begin to jump from one thing to another, seemingly totally unrelated.

It is important to simply let these thoughts flow while in the Theta state.

As you continue with your meditation practice, you will find yourself becoming more adept at taking an observer position with your conscious mind; this is when you begin to reap the benefits of accessing your subconscious mind through meditation.

By definition, relaxation refers to [1] relief from bodily or mental work (effort, application).

Relaxation can also refer to [2] an activity or recreation that provides such relief, thereby creating a diversion and/or a form of entertainment.

Living The ED Principles

When faced with numerous responsibilities, tasks and demands, relaxation often takes a back seat in our lives.

Relaxation reduces stress symptoms by [1] slowing your heart rate, [2] lowering your blood pressure, [3] slowing your breathing rate, [4] increasing blood flow to the major muscles, [5] reducing muscle tension and chronic pain, [6] improving concentration, [7] reducing anger and frustration, and [8] boosting confidence to handle problems

Relaxation, in conjunction with exercise, getting enough sleep, and reaching out to supportive family and friends, is also essential.

Meditation can certainly be one way to relax.

Breathing deeply, a favorite of mine, is one whereby you experience immediate results.

By focusing solely on the breath, you take your concentration away from that which has angered you, upset you, or distressed you, in some way.

Inhale through your nose, feeling the breath start in your abdomen and work its way to the top of your head; exhale through your mouth.

Being present in the now is another favorite way to relax; simply stop and take stock of everything around you (how it looks, how it feels, how it smells, how it tastes).

Talking to others (preferably face-to-face or at least on the phone) is a great way to manage whatever is stressing you out.

Laughing is a relaxation technique that needs to be utilized more often (as a Type A personality, I am speaking from personal experience).

A hearty laugh serves to lighten the mental load that a great many of us continue to carry about.

It also helps to lower cortisol (the stress hormone produced by your body) while increasing endorphins (chemicals in the brain) that help to boost your mood.

You can easily lighten up by tuning in to your favorite sitcom or video, reading the comics, chatting with someone who makes you smile or listening to your favorite music.

Soothing music can lower blood pressure, heart rate and anxiety. From my own personal collection, I love to listen to the sounds of nature (the ocean, a bubbling brook, a waterfall, birds chirping).

All forms of exercise can ease depression and anxiety by helping the brain release those feel-good chemicals; so, too, does exercise give your body a chance to practice dealing with stress.

Living The ED Principles

Expressing gratitude is yet another relaxation technique.

Every time you demonstrate gratitude for the blessings in your life, these positives serve to cancel out the negative thoughts and worries.

Simply put, there is no single relaxation technique that works for everyone.

If you have a tendency to become angry, or agitated, in reaction to stress, you may find that meditation, deep breathing, or guided imagery (visualization) work best because they serve to quiet you down.

If you have a tendency to react to stress by becoming depressed and withdrawn, you may find that respond best to relaxation techniques that stimulate and energize your nervous system, such as rhythmic exercise. Aerobic exercise boosts oxygen circulation, triggering your body to make feel-good chemicals (endorphins).

If you have a tendency to eat in reaction to stress, you need to identify the foods that will reduce your stress levels.

Complex carbohydrates (whole-grain breakfast cereals, breads, and pastas, as well as old-fashioned oatmeal) serve to boost levels of serotonin, a calming brain chemical; so, too, do they help you feel balanced by stabilizing your blood sugar levels.

Vitamin C can curb levels of stress hormones while strengthening your immune system at the same time.

Other foods can cut levels of cortisol and adrenaline, the stress hormones that take a toll on the body over time.

Too little magnesium can trigger headaches and fatigue, further compounding the effects of stress. You can replenish your magnesium stores quite easily, by eating spinach (as in a salad), cooked soybeans or a filet of salmon.

Omega-3 fatty acids, found in fish such as salmon and tuna, can prevent surges in stress hormones.

The drinking of black tea may help you recover from stressful events more quickly. By comparison, when it comes to stress, the caffeine in coffee can boost stress hormones and raise blood pressure.

Almonds serve to assist you in becoming more resilient during bouts of stress, such as depression.

Eating raw vegetables can help ease stress; the munching of celery or carrot sticks helps release a clenched jaw, which serves to ease tension.

Ingesting carbohydrates at bedtime can speed the release of the brain chemical serotonin, helping you sleep better; at this time, it is always best to stick to something light, such as toast and jam.

Guided Meditation

Many studies show that practicing something in your mind is almost as effective as practicing in real life.

Everything that you experience, in your day to day living, serves to create neural pathways in the brain.

If you take the time to think of your mind as an MP3 player, there are hundreds of songs (programs) available to you, for immediate download, at any time.

We already know that these programs are stored in the subconscious mind.

Were you aware, however, that they are also stored in the very cells of your body?

If you take the time to ponder on the ramifications of this last statement, you come to understand that our genes do not determine who we are.

Living The ED Principles

By the very nature of this premise, it becomes the images that we create in our minds, of ourselves, that determines who we are.

With the thousands of programs that exist, written into our subconscious mind, each one governs how we think, act and behave in any situation.

We cannot change any of these programs without some means of access to the subconscious mind, whereby the programs need to be rewritten.

Along with effective change, new neural pathways are created, pathways that communicate with the cells and genes in our bodies.

Guided meditation has the power to reach the subconscious mind through images and sounds to create an experience that simulates a lived (real) experience.

Guided Meditation involves being verbally guided, by a narrator, into a state of consciousness that elicits a specific change in your life. To assist you in the reaching of a deep meditative state, you are first guided to relax your body and mind. Thereafter, the journey begins; a journey within the mind to reach a specific goal.

The beauty of a guided meditation is that you can bring about a change in your body by using your mind. This process actually involves activating your muscles and changing your biological state, which also changes the way the cells in your body work.

Visualization

Visualization (or creative visualization as some term it) simply involves learning to use your imagination to create clear visual images, ideas or feelings (through sensing) in a more conscious way; as one continues to focus on the image (idea, feeling) in a positive way, the energy results in the creation of that imagined reality.

What you focus on, you attract.

We live in a quantum sea of vibrating energy; an incredible energy that is always responding to how we think and what we think.

Our thoughts and feelings are creative forces.

Even though the subconscious mind cannot distinguish between what is real and what is imagined, it will act upon the images that you create, whether they reflect your current reality or not.

Living The ED Principles

This is where visualization comes into play.

There is a mental trick to visualization; you need to live and feel as if you *already have* what you want.

As long as you continue to persist in your vision, you will achieve what you want.

Visualization is one of the most significant keys to success; actively picturing yourself achieving a goal will help you actually achieve it.

Visualization + Emotion + Repetition + Inspired Action = Abundance

When you visualize, you must see (hear, feel, smell, taste, touch) everything in vivid detail, taking the time to spend at least 15 minutes each day engaged thusly.

You *need* to be able to envision your dream. When you take the time to visualize, the things you are imagining seem to be magnetically drawn to you.

Living The ED Principles

Napoleon Hill, author of <u>Think and Grow Rich,</u> has this to say ... *Our brains become magnetized with the dominating thoughts we hold in our minds, and, by means with which no man is familiar, these 'magnets' attract to us the forces, thepeople, the circumstances of life which harmonize with the nature of our dominating thoughts.*

Our mind and thoughts produce energy.

Energy always follows thought and feeling.

Thoughts are always birthed in the spiritual realm, first, before they are reproduced in the manifested physical realm of our existence.

Visualization, then, changes you physically, energetically and spiritually in that you are affected on all three levels *anytime you imagine with feeling.*

I like to avail of the <u>Everyday Visualization System</u> created by my good friend Carl Harvey (refer to the Bibliography).

Living The ED Principles

Carl literally takes you by the hand and shows you exactly how to use his five-step formula systematic system to easily (and quickly) create powerful visualizations that get big results.

Relaxing deep into the Alpha state (as per Carl's program) is what gives you better access to your subconscious mind.

You need to create a sensory rich image of what you want to experience; sights, sounds and feelings are particularly important avenues.

You need to envision each goal as vividly as you can; as you see it happening in your mind's eye, making it as real as you can, for this is what builds expectation.

You must believe it will happen, just as you have imagined it.

You must expect it to happen, just as you have imagined it.

You must trust it to happen, just as you have imagined it.

Living The ED Principles

The more you trust the process, the faster your desire will find you.

I also like to avail of guided visualizations that have already been created, by Carl, for me to use (refer to the <u>8 Minute Manifesting</u> program located in the Bibliography).

One of the common misconceptions about visualization is that you need to be a master at "seeing" crystal-clear images inside your imagination; this is simply not true.

The process is all about *how good the visualization feels*, not how it looks.

In fact, the key is to generate the positive emotions you expect to experience when you manifest your goal.

Paradoxically, it is the intensity of the feeling this seems to attract opportunities, people and circumstances to you.

As you spend time visualizing each day, you will begin to feel an emotional shift, the cue that you have been waiting for; this is the sign that you are now broadcasting a new vibrational signal.

The longer you are able to hold this new vibration, the faster your reality will shift.

As already eluded to, there are three necessary elements to successful visualization.

DESIRE = *I have the desire to create* what I have hereby chosen to visualize.

BELIEF = *I believe in my goal* and have the confidence that I will achieve it (or something better).

ACCEPTANCE = *I accept my vision* and will continue to pursue it with the full intention of bringing it to fruition.

Living The ED Principles

If we always get from life what we think about, as the saying goes, do take the time to follow (and work towards achieving) these suggestions ……..

º Refuse to accept limiting beliefs.

º Work on eliminating limiting beliefs.

º Visualize your dream in vivid, sensory rich detail; knowing that your subconscious mind cannot tell the difference between a real memory and a vividly imagined one, take the time to use all of your senses when you visualize.

º See what you will see.

º Hear what you will hear.

º Feel how good it feels to have everything you dream of, and more, in an easy and relaxed manner, in a healthy and positive way.

Here is what Jack Canfield has to say about visualization.

If we can believe in some of the newer theories of quantum physics, visualizing your desires will send out waves of energy that will attract the people and resources to you that you need to accomplish your goals.

Here is what Bob Proctor, creator of <u>The Science of Getting Rich</u> has to share about visualization.

When you hold the image of your goal on the screen of your mind, in the present tense, you are vibrating in harmony with every particle of energy necessary for the manifestation of your image on the physical plane.

By holding that image, those particles of energy are moving toward you (attraction) and you are moving toward them, because that is the law.

It also needs to be shared that my good friend Carl Harvey has this to add to Bob's words.

The ability to hold the image of what you want probably isn't enough for you to manifest it.

Yes, you should do everything you can to stimulate an intense, burning desire for whatever you want to create, manifest and experience more of.

You should certainly visualize every day, because in time you will rid yourself of ideas of lack and scarcity, growing more confident.

But the real keystone to manifesting is not simply holding a vision of what you want. It is BELIEF.

Possessing a deep, self belief is as rare and compelling as a bird of paradise. REAL belief is attractive, magnetic, and almost impossible to resist.

Having Belief is what attracts the "magic" of synchronicity and flow.

Listen To Your Intuition

Your subconscious mind has a way of warning you, of dangers as well as opportunities, before your conscious mind has access to all of the information; this is called your intuition.

When you are trying to make a decision (whereby you may be confronted with a problem), the very first thought response that probably comes to the forefront of your conscious mind is probably your subconscious talking to you.

When this happens, you are not able to explain why you feel this way or why you think it is the right decision.

What is absolutely fascinating, however, is that these decisions, made in the blink of an eye, are usually incredibly perceptive and astonishingly accurate.

If you have ever experienced déjà vu (the phenomenon of having the strong sensation that an event currently being experienced was experienced in the past) in keeping with a person or a place, you have experienced your subconscious trying to make contact with you.

If you have ever experienced a sudden, strong intuition about something that was going to happen, you have experienced your subconscious trying to make contact with you.

If you have ever experienced a gnawing sensation in your gut (that things are not going right), despite the fact that, on the surface, everything seems to be fine, you have experienced your subconscious trying to make contact with you.

If you have ever been made uncomfortable by someone you have just met, someone who seems friendly enough, you have experienced your subconscious trying to make contact with you, perhaps to warn you of some deeper anger or angst.

Living The ED Principles

In moments such as these, it is imperative to listen to your subconscious mind.

So, too, would it be even more beneficial to make friends with your subconscious, listening to it whenever you want to figure out what someone is intending to do (or thinking), whether in a meeting, a negotiation or simply a conversation with a friend.

As you take the time to practice your listening skills, so, too, will your abilities to hear your subconscious, quickly and accurately, steadily improve.

So, too, are we able to pose intuitive questions to the subconscious mind, courtesy of muscle testing. [27] [28] [29]

---

[27] http://www.formulaformiracles.net/muscle-testing.html
[28] https://theawareshow.com/2011/brent-phillips/tas-attract-brent-phillips-special-02-science-meets-spirit.pdf
[29] http://www.eftstatements.com/articles/muscle-testing/

Arm Lever Method [30]

Finger Ring Method [31]

Pendulum Method [32]

Standing Method [33]

---

[30] https://www.youtube.com/watch?v=GRRDh1CS-4o
[31] https://www.youtube.com/watch?v=uLPPlipLmjk
[32] https://www.youtube.com/watch?v=oMhzh67th1M
[33] https://www.youtube.com/watch?v=9h066iN-V8I

Thought Field Therapy

Thought Field Therapy (TFT), a sequential tapping procedure, as discovered by the now deceased Dr. Roger Callahan, provides a code to nature's healing system.

Applied to problems, TFT addresses the fundamental causes, thereby balancing the body's energy system, allowing you to eliminate most negative emotions (or fears) within minutes; this makes TFT tapping a highly effective, non-invasive, healthy self-help alternative to long-term, or drug-related, psychotherapy.

Thought Field Therapy has been used for [1] trauma relief, [2] elimination of fears, anxiety and stress, [3] successful weight loss, [4] smoking cessation, and [5] easing the weight of depression without medications.

As well, TFT also offers advanced EFT (Emotional Freedom Technique) Algorithms to help one overcome specific challenges.

Living The ED Principles

According to the website, [34] expanding on EFT claims, the sequence of meridian points does matter; once reversals are identified and cleared, the correct meridian sequence will often result in dramatic drops in experienced distress.

The common sequences, which can be used without the skilled diagnostic procedure, are called algorithms; many of these are described in Dr Callahan's book, <u>Tapping the Healer Within</u>.

Dr. Callahan considers 'psychological reversal' to be one of his most important discoveries; while also addressed in EFT, they are given less emphasis than in TFT, where they can be detected and corrected with observable results. [35]

Thought Field Tapping Therapy is a field of information, expressed in the body's energy system, generated by the thought in the mind.

---

[34] http://www.rogercallahan.com/index.php
[35] Ibid.

Living The ED Principles

This formulation is subtly different from the EFT idea of a blockage in the energy system.

If a person learns only EFT, then he or she may be unaware of some important details that are taught within TFT.

These complexities and subtleties are discussed by Ian Graham, of the British Thought Field Therapy Association, who has compiled a detailed account of differences between TFT and EFT. [36] [37]

---

[36] http://www.drng.net/EFTvs.TFT.htm
[37] http://www.rogercallahan.com/news/tft-in-the-uk/thought-field-therapy

EFT Tapping

Meridian tapping, a combination of ancient Chinese acupressure and modern psychology, involves tapping with your fingertips on specific points (meridian points) on your face and upper body, while repeating selected statements out loud.

There are meridian pathways, throughout your body, through which energy flows. By tapping, you are sending an electrical signal through the body that clears the energy blockages (stuck energies), allowing the energy to flow freely again.

So, too, are you able to ease emotional and physical pains that may be symptoms of anxiety and stress, fears and phobias, performance blocks, post traumatic stress, and deep rooted issues from your childhood (all of which can result in limited beliefs and self-sabotage).

Living The ED Principles

EFT (Emotional Freedom Techniques) [38]

EFT Tapping: Energy Morse Code [39]

EFT Tapping Points [40]

FREE EFT Videos [41]

Tapping International [42]

The Energy Therapy Centre [43]

The Tapping Solution (Nick Ortner) [44] [45]

---

[38] http://www.eftuniverse.com/
[39] http://www.healing-with-eft.com/eft-tapping.html
[40] http://www.tapintoeft.com/eft-tapping-points/
[41] http://www.tapping.com/videos.html
[42] http://www.tappinginternational.com/
[43] http://www.theenergytherapycentre.co.uk/tapping-points.htm
[44] http://www.thetappingsolution.com/
[45] http://www.thetappingsolution.com/eft-articles/nick-ortner/

Meridian Tapping Techniques

The purpose of Meridian Tapping Techniques (MTT) is to recognize and appreciate the variety of methods which have the person tap on, or otherwise utilize, meridian points.

Meridian Tapping Techniques is a generic term; as a result, it cannot be registered or trademarked, meaning that it is therefore open to all.

The MTT website [46] was founded to act as an expansive community that encompasses all meridian-based therapies and interventions, including Emotional Freedom Techniques (EFT), Thought Field Therapy (TFT), and others.

The goal of the MTT website is to provide resources, support, services, affiliations, a general organization and "meeting place" for those who want to explore meridian tapping techniques; so, too, is it a place for those who want to spread the word in a variety of different ways.

---

[46] http://www.meridiantappingtechniques.com/

Ho'oponopono

Ho'oponopono (ho-o-pono-pono) is an ancient Hawaiian practice for reconciliation and forgiveness that provides a way to release the energy of painful thoughts, thereafter creating increased health, abundance and peace in your life.

Ho'oponopono means *to make right*.

Originally used in family situations where there was disharmony among family members, a mediator would be invited and Ho'oponopono would be used to make things right between them.

In 1976, Morrnah Simeona began to modify the traditional Hawaiian forgiveness and reconciliation process of Ho'oponopono to include the realities of the modern day, calling this Self-Identity through Ho'oponopono. [47]

---

[47] http://being-free.com/images/stories/docs/The%20Twelve%20steps%20of%20Hooponopono%20PDF.pdf

Living The ED Principles

This is an extremely simple strategy that, in its most basic form, involves you "cleaning" yourself by saying four simple phrases:

I'm sorry, Please forgive me, Thank you, I love you.

You say these phrases to yourself, silently if you wish. This seems rather too simplistic, yet the results can often be profound and life changing when people master the art of Ho'oponopono.

One of the most common experiences is that Ho'oponopono clears out bad programming in your subconscious mind, helping to eliminate old limiting beliefs and negative programming that has prevented you from getting what you want out of life, which also includes achieving the success that you strive for.

In finding yourself more open to receiving inspiration from the Divine, you take effortless inspired action, bringing an increased flow of abundance into all areas of your life.

Robert F. Ray, author of <u>Return to Zeropoint II: Ho'oponopono for a Better Reality</u>, and a very dear friend of mine, offers workshops and seminars in how to utilize the principles of Ho'oponopono for emotional healing.

Ancient Hawaiian Ho'oponopono App [48]

History of Ho'oponopono [49]

Subliminal Clearing: Z Plus Advanced Ho'oponopono [50]

---

[48] http://hooponopono.wrhmedia.com/
[49] http://soultransync.com/history-of-hooponopono/
[50] http://www.subliminalclearing.com/

Raise Your Vibration

Each and every time you raise your vibration, you invite something better into your life.

There exists a direct correlation between one's level of raised vibration and their level of success.

A really easy way to raise your vibration is to imagine what you want to experience, in as much detail as you can.

Focusing on what you want makes you feel good; it also helps to program your subconscious for success.

Focusing on what you want makes you feel confident, happy, inspired.

Your true vibration is what you are broadcasting outwardly to the universe.

Too often the vibration you believe you are broadcasting for all to hear does not even come close to matching the vibration that you are actually putting out.

Living The ED Principles

Your mannerisms and your choice of words are always a clue to your true vibration.

Learning to sense and control the vibrational frequencies that you are emitting is quite the challenge.

Awaken Your Spirit

The Dalai Lama, when asked what surprised him most about humanity, answered ……

Man because he sacrifices his health to make money.

Then he sacrifices money to recuperate his health.

And then he is so anxious about the future that he does not enjoy the present; the result being that he does not live in the present or the future.

He lives as if he is never going to die, and then dies having never really lived.

Live Fearlessly

What lies behind us and what lies before us are tiny matters compared to what lies within us. Ralph Waldo Emerson

Too many people get caught up in their negative thinking, always expecting doom and gloom in their lives.

When they get exactly what they expected to get, they say something along the lines of *I just knew something like this would happen to me because I've always had bad luck.*

This is what is called creating your own reality experience.

You are the captain of the ship; the ship, of course, being your conscious mind.

Your thoughts, beliefs and expectations provide the direction that your life will take.

Living The ED Principles

This means that if you want to change the direction you are headed towards, you must first change the thoughts, beliefs and expectations that are leading you there.

Most times, a simple shift in your perception can create positive change, allowing you to see opportunities that you may not have been able to entertain before (as even being remotely possible).

Our subconscious mind is always awake, monitoring our thoughts; it never sleeps. That having been said, the subconscious mind is aware of every thought, taking notice of our most persistent thoughts and beliefs, as well as our expectations.

Once it becomes clear as to what those persistent thoughts and beliefs are, it diligently goes to work to attract those very things into your life.

Too many times we become fearful over what we imagine might happen.

This fearful living disables our ability to live in the here and now, despite the fact that the fear is naught but an internal one.

This is when it becomes important to realize that all you can ever control is the action (thoughts, words, deeds) that you take.

By comparison, to live fearlessly means to live with integrity.

I do my best to live in this way.

In presenting myself to others, I am exactly who I say I am; so, too, do I conduct myself in this same manner.

Living The ED Principles

Fearless living also means living in the moment.

This is when it can be said that you are living in total harmony with the essence of who you are.

Responding, not reacting, becomes a highlight of this approach, allowing you to speak your truth, not your fears.

Knowing that we get in life what we habitually expect to get, you must learn to *expect only the best*.

Change Is Necessary For Growth

By definition, change usually refers to a transformation (or modification) from the original state, the supplanting of one thing by another; hence, change is a deviation.

As truthfully proposed by Heraclitus, *nothing is constant except change*, for it is ever present and inherent in our world.

As human beings we like to act as if life will, and should, always be predictable, and yet we know this to be false.

We often feel offended by change because we are creatures of habit.

As logical as we try our best to be, we are emotional human beings.

Change often brings upset, disturbance and irritation to the fore; feelings we would rather not have to deal with.

Living The ED Principles

Too often, we fear what we do not know.

As a result, the normal human experience, for the most part, relates to attempting to keep everything in a familiar state.

Transformation is all about change and change is not the least bit familiar; if it were, it would not be change.

Therein lies the irony, for when one does their best to avoid change, at all costs, so, too, is one running away from what they may want the most; namely, transformation.

You are the creator.

You are the progenitor of what you receive.

You are also the begetter of what you experience.

Fear is not to be avoided; instead, it needs to be welcomed into your life. There is always a reason as to why fear presents itself; this is what needs to be further investigated.

Living The ED Principles

As soon as we begin to realize that change is not something to be feared and/or avoided, this is when we can finally learn to let go of the fear of change.

When embraced, change keeps us moving, change keeps us motivated, change keeps us interested.

If we do not change, we do not grow; quite simply put, we continue to stagnate amidst a dull and boring existence.

Within the confines of an unchanging, albeit cozy, lifestyle, one will never get to experience the incredible vastness of diversity that exists.

We are here to live life with passion.

We are here to live life with intent.

We are here to live life with joy and enthusiasm.

Living The ED Principles

Personal change is a reflection of one's inner growth and empowerment.

Change takes time; you must remember to be patient with yourself.

Change requires vigilance; you must remember to persist as you do your utmost to *keep on keeping on.*

Change necessitates the ability to overcome setbacks; as a result, you need to maintain your motivation and confidence in the face of periodic failures and disappointment; this is what we refer to as perseverance.

The words of Marcus Aurelius Antoninus serve to put things in perspective ... *The universe is change; our life is what our thoughts make it.*

Gratitude

To be in vibrational alignment, you must ensure that you are making (or have already made) changes to your physical reality so that you can experience more of what it is that you truly want to experience in your life.

When I speak of making changes to your physical reality, this can first be accomplished through the changes you make within your consciousness, after which they ripple outwards, automatically filtering to your outer world.

As we continue to battle a life filled with stress and tension, too often we fail to see what is right before our eyes.

In taking the time to notice, on a conscious basis, what you appreciate (what you feel grateful for, what you feel good about), it becomes in the deepening of those feelings that you will find your physical reality changing to represent a life that you can enjoy.

Living The ED Principles

Take the time to appreciate breathing, the first miracle we have all been blessed with.

Take the time to appreciate beauty it all of its many unique forms (sunset, sunrise, moon, stars).

Take the time to appreciate nature (the colors, the textures, the landscapes).

Take the time to appreciate warmth and security.

Take the time to appreciate companionship.

Take the time to appreciate the five physical senses that allow you experience your physical reality.

Take the time to appreciate the wonder (and endurance levels) of the physical body.

Take the time to appreciate the full gamut of emotions that are available to you, so that you may experience the vastness and richness of life, so that you may grow and learn as an individual.

Living The ED Principles

As you learn to take the time to appreciate the totality of life without resistance (especially if you know and believe that something better exists around the corner), this is what enables your desire(s) to become the dominant energetic signal(s) that you are broadcasting to the conscious universe.

Once you have made this internal shift, you will discover that your outer reality also improves, mainly because you are experiencing increased vibrational alignment (harmony) within your inner world.

When your inner world and outer world become the same world, this is when you experience vibrational alignment (harmony, oneness).

If ever you do not like what you see in your outer word, you must [1] change the signal that you are broadcasting, first and foremost, and [2] work through, and release, the resistance (that you may be feeling) about your desired new reality.

Living The ED Principles

Given the nonjudgmental and conscious nature of the universe, your outer world will continue to rearrange itself to keep pace with your awakened consciousness.

Do What You Love

What is it that makes you feel alive?

What stirs your passion?

What makes you feel empowered?

When you do what you love, you are in a position to be able to inspire others to do what they love.

When you do what you love, you add value to the world.

You are limited only by [1] your imagination and [2] your fear of failure.

In fact, it was Thomas Edison who said *I have not failed. I have just found 10,000 ways that didn't work.*

Living The ED Principles

Let's face it, as humans we have an inner desire to express ourselves, to expand and create.

When we do something that we are intrinsically motivated to do, we bring our gift(s) to the world.

While the extrinsic stuff might pay more financially, so that you can eke out a living for yourself and your family, it can also rob you of happiness.

Rich Fernandez, in his article *Life's Work*, [51] shares the following:

[1] Instead of creating "To Do" lists for ourselves, we need to be creating "To Be" lists, based on what we aspire to be in our working lives and beyond.

° How would I like each day to unfold?

51

http://communicate.eckharttolle.com/news/2013/06/20/lifes-work/

Living The ED Principles

° What would I like to be focusing my energy and attention on, if I had any choice available to me?

° What makes me experience joy?

° What energizes me?

° What makes me feel balance?

° What makes me feel integration?

° What state of mind would I like to be in while I work?

° What other aspects of my life do I wish to be paying more attention to?

°By the end of my life, what kind of person do I wish to be?

[2] The answers that emerge from questions like these can influence and direct your work, ultimately allowing you to thrive in that work because you are following your own life's energy, instead of opposing it, fighting it or suppressing it.

Living The ED Principles

[3] By placing attention to what it means to be fully aligned (fully yourself, fully present in your work), you are able to give your best to your work, to yourself *and* to the world.

The only words that I can add to these are thank you, Rich, for these wonderful insights.

Let the beauty of what you love be what you do. Rumi

Doing what you love is the cornerstone of having abundance in your life. Wayne Dyer

Are you bored with life? Then throw yourself into some work you believe in with all your heart, live for it, die for it, and you will find happiness that you had thought could never be yours. Dale Carnegie

Living The ED Principles

In dwelling, live close to the ground. In thinking, keep to the simple. In conflict, be fair and generous. In governing, don't try to control. In work, do what you enjoy. In family life, be completely present. Lao Tzu

If there is no passion in your life, then have you really lived? Find your passion, whatever it may be. Become it, and let it become you and you will find great things happen for you, to you and because of you. Alan Armstrong

Once you make a decision, the universe conspires to make it happen. Emerson

If one advances confidently in the direction of one's dreams, and endeavours to live the life which one has imagined, one will meet with a success unexpected in common hours. Henry David Thoreau

Living The ED Principles

The Holstee Manifesto (located on the following page) [52] is an eloquent and beautifully written dissertation to the life of purpose, the life of passion and the life of productivity.

In doing what you love, so, too, are you embracing your real and authentic self.

By allowing your own light to shine, you give others permission, courtesy of your example, to do the same.

In the embracingof your authenticity, know that you will continue to attract people, and experiences, that will be as real and authentic as yourself.

---

[52] http://shop.holstee.com/?campaignid=446&mbsy=7pD

Living The ED Principles

THIS IS YOUR LIFE.
DO WHAT YOU LOVE, AND DO IT OFTEN.
IF YOU DON'T LIKE SOMETHING, CHANGE IT.
IF YOU DON'T LIKE YOUR JOB, QUIT.
IF YOU DON'T HAVE ENOUGH TIME, STOP WATCHING TV.
IF YOU ARE LOOKING FOR THE LOVE OF YOUR LIFE, STOP;
THEY WILL BE WAITING FOR YOU WHEN YOU
START DOING THINGS YOU LOVE.
STOP OVER ANALYZING, ALL EMOTIONS ARE BEAUTIFUL.
LIFE IS SIMPLE. WHEN YOU EAT, APPRECIATE EVERY LAST BITE.
OPEN YOUR MIND, ARMS, AND HEART TO NEW THINGS AND PEOPLE, WE ARE UNITED IN OUR DIFFERENCES.
ASK THE NEXT PERSON YOU SEE WHAT THEIR PASSION IS, AND SHARE YOUR INSPIRING DREAM WITH THEM.
TRAVEL OFTEN; GETTING LOST WILL HELP YOU FIND YOURSELF.
SOME OPPORTUNITIES ONLY COME ONCE, SEIZE THEM.
LIFE IS ABOUT THE PEOPLE YOU MEET, AND THE THINGS YOU CREATE WITH THEM SO GO OUT AND START CREATING.
LIFE IS SHORT. LIVE YOUR DREAM AND SHARE YOUR PASSION.

"THE HOLSTEE MANIFESTO" ©2009   WRITTEN BY DAVE, MIKE & FABIAN   DESIGN BY RACHAEL   WWW.HOLSTEE.COM/MANIFESTO

In doing what you love, while the money may not always follow, you *will* enjoy your life.

In doing what you love, while the money may not always follow, you *will* feel fulfilled.

In doing what you love, while the money may not always follow, happiness *will* reign supreme.

In doing what you love, the money will seem less relevant.

The world needs more people who are 'living' in the truest sense of the word; the sad reality is that doing what you love is the dream of many, but the real world of very few.

As has been shared in <u>The Peaceful Warrior</u> by Dan Millman ... *A warrior does not give up what he loves. He finds the love in what he does.*

Living The ED Principles

Finding the love in what you do (in all aspects of your life) might well be the best way to move forward in today's career path.

In truth, it is all about mindfulness.

Marsha Sinetar is the author of <u>Do What You Love, The Money Will Follow: Discovering Your Right Livelihood</u>, a tome wherein she makes the argument "for a cohesiveness between love, work and play, and finding a way to express yourself through a fully-lived life." [53]

Seeing the value of balance, compromise and choice, Sinetar carefully notes "that the money doesn't just follow: we must do the work first, invest in ourselves, and gradually see the results of our efforts." [54]

---

[53] http://www.psychologytoday.com/blog/career-transitions/201211/can-you-really-do-what-you-love-these-days
[54] Ibid.

Sinetar also focuses on what she terms *right livelihood*, meaning "the ability to craft a vocation that is authentic; a concept that fits nicely with the latest findings in positive psychology." [55]

Take a few minutes, right now, and ask yourself if you have found your right livelihood.

Are you pursuing what you love?

If not, have you been able to find the love in what you do?

Seen from the positive perspective, there will always be ways to *incorporate what you love into what you do*.

In truth, your right livelihood is something that will continue to evolve.

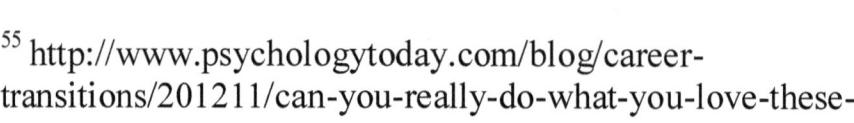

---

[55] http://www.psychologytoday.com/blog/career-transitions/201211/can-you-really-do-what-you-love-these-days

Living The ED Principles

I think true passion is your greatest economic security.
Tama Kieves

As far as advice goes, here is what Tama [56] has to say.

[1] Take your pulse; if you are energized by the path you are choosing, such as writing, then you know you are headed in the right direction.

[2] Do not try to define it right away. Look for something you love and then let your instincts guide you; be willing to let it evolve.

[3] Stop planning; no one can plan an inspired life. You will know when it is right because it feels so peaceful.

[4] Stop listening to doubters, for fear will sound too much like practicality. You are here to follow the love. There is a reason that you have this desire; there is a reason why this dream is speaking to you.

56

http://www.usatoday.com/story/money/columnist/bruzzese/2013/08/25/on-the-job-inspired-work/2690443/

Living The ED Principles

Clearly, it is imperative, then, that one follow their genius, their talent and their dream, all courtesy of inspired action and firm belief.

Jonathan Mead writes that "the greatest change happens because of people that are deeply passionate, and have a great love for the work they do. If you want to make a difference in the world, the single most important thing you can do is consciously, and deliberately, choose to do work that you are passionate about; no other choice can have a greater impact on the planet, or your life." [57]

According to Jonathan, here is the summarized (and paraphrased) plan[58] that you must follow.

[1] You need to identify your passion. What is it that makes you feel energized? What is it that makes you come alive? What is it that you could talk about for hours on end?

---

[57] http://zenhabits.net/the-world-needs-you-to-do-what-you-love/
[58] Ibid.

[2] You need to identify your strengths. What is it that you are naturally good at? When other people talk about your talents, what do they say?

[3] You need to identify your value, meaning that you must find the convergence that exists between what you are good at and what people are willing to pay you for.

[4] You need to be committed to working at what you are passionate about.

[5] You must be willing to let go of old (and outdated) thought and behavior patterns as you work your way towards a new direction.

[6] You must make time for your new journey, meaning that you must be willing to give up something in order to achieve that which is your passion.

[7] You must own your passion, completely and without reservation, giving yourself permission to call yourself a writer, a painter, a life coach, even if you are not yet fully established.

Living The ED Principles

Steve Harrison talks about the fact that it is always uncomfortable to *claim your expertise*, which is exactly what Jonathan is alluding to.

You must never take for granted what it is that you know.

You must never take for granted the value of what it is that you know.

Never, ever, sell yourself short; you may have information to help people solve a problem.

You may be able to help people achieve something that they really want to achieve.

You may be able to help people overcome a serious problem that they want to overcome.

We all know that whenever you do something new for the very first time, even when following your passion, it always feels uncomfortable.

As long as you are willing to feel uncomfortable, as long as you are willing to embrace this change, rest assured in knowing that this is how you will grow as an individual.

In accordance with the wisdom of comedian Steve Martin, who once said, *be so good, they can't ignore you*, we must never stop growing and developing our effectiveness, our competence, our potentialities and our qualifications.

In the words of Paramahansa Yogananda ... *life is to be lived. If you live abundantly and use all your talents and energies to the limit every day, you'll develop ever-greater power and understanding of your full potential as a soul. There's no end to the life, love, power and wisdom that could be yours if you start using what you have.*

The Power of the Mind

As you have been able to see, courtesy of the earlier chapters of this book, mind is the matrix of all matter in that your mind can actually influence matter, which is the quantum field of pure potentiality (the same malleable substance that Napoleon Hill references; likewise for Albert Einstein).

Purely as a demonstrative example, money has its own energy.

We all have beliefs associated with money.

These beliefs can only do one of two things: they will either create an energy that attracts money or they will create an energy that repels money.

The secret, then, to attracting more money, is to change your vibration so that it matches the vibration associated with money (which is always neutral).

Unfortunately many of our beliefs about money operate on a subconscious level; once accepted, they serve to become reality.

Limiting Belief = Money is the root of all evil.

Empowering Belief = Money is a resource that allows me to give, to create, to share and to uplift others.

Limiting Belief = The rich get richer, and the poor get poorer.

Empowering Belief = Abundance, which exists all around me, is there for everyone.

Limiting Belief = Money is a limited resource.

Empowering Belief = Living within an infinite (limitless) universe, there can never be a shortage of money.

Living The ED Principles

Limiting Belief = I have to work exceptionally hard to be wealthy.

Empowering Belief = I accumulate wealth, courtesy of utmost honesty and integrity.

Limiting Belief = Money is not important.

Empowering Belief = I feel positive about money and all of the good that it continues to bring into my life.

While your beliefs are not your reality, they do serve to co-create your reality experience, meaning that you must eliminate limiting beliefs so that you can replace them with empowering ones.

In so doing, you are taking complete responsibility for your life.

In the words of Siddhārtha Gautama, more commonly known as Buddha ... *To enjoy good health, to bring true happiness to one's family, to bring peace to all, one must first discipline and control one's own mind. If a man can control his mind he can find the way to Enlightenment, and all wisdom and virtue will naturally come to him.*

In the words of Khalil Gibran, author of The Prophet ... *The teacher who is indeed wise does not bid you to enter the house of his wisdom, but rather leads you to the threshold of your mind.*

So, too, did Khalil Gibran state ... *Your living is determined not so much by what life brings to you as by the attitude you bring to life; not so much by what happens to you as by the way your mind looks at what happens.*

As spoken by Aristotle ... *The energy of the mind is the essence of life.*

Living The ED Principles

That having been said, knowing that we have the power to change our deep rooted beliefs (thoughts, perceptions and feelings), which further impacts our actions, is a gift of monumental proportion.

According to Robert Collier, author of <u>Secret of the Ages</u> ... *every condition, every experience of life is the result of our mental attitude. We can* do *only what we think we can do. We can* be *only what we think we can be. We can* have *only what we think we can have. What we do, what we are, what we have, all depend upon what we think. We can never express anything that we do not first have in mind. The secret of all power, all success, all riches, is in first thinking powerful thoughts, successful thoughts, thoughts of wealth, of supply. We must build them in our own mind first.* [59]

The central tenet here is to *focus* on what you want.

---

[59] http://www.sacred-texts.com/nth/tsoa/tsoa08.htm (pages 82 and 83)

Robert Collier also cites Baudouin when he shares that *there is no philosophy which will help a man to succeed when he is always doubting his ability to do so, and thus attracting failure.*[60]

In other words, if you expect to fail, you shall most assuredly fail, but if you expect to succeed, then you can achieve anything you set your mind to.

We create our lives through our own thought processes.

Everything you think, you will feel.

Everything you feel, you will manifest.

Everything you manifest serves to create the condition(s) of your life.

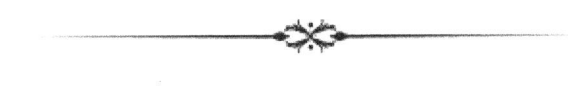

---

[60] http://www.sacred-texts.com/nth/tsoa/tsoa08.htm (page 97)

Living The ED Principles

Every word you utter expresses some feeling within your soul.

Every word you utter serves to create the condition(s) of your life.

Herein lies the direct fusion of thought with emotion.

You *become* what you think.

You *become* what you believe.

You *become* what you speak.

Therein lies the power of your mind; thinking and believing are key.

Individuals are capable of accomplishing great feats using the power of the mind; acknowledging this power, and using it constructively and effectively, is what enables them to live plentiful and satisfied lives.

Living The ED Principles

In order to program your mind to do what you want it to do, [1] you first have to understand the subconscious mind and how it works; thereafter, [2] you must learn how to control the subconscious mind (so you can reprogram it), for only then will you have the ability to reach the empowered levels that your mind can achieve for you.

Developing your understanding of the power of the mind starts with knowing two laws or principles; namely, The Law of Vibration and The Law of Attraction.

What Do You Believe?

Every time we have a conversation, see something, hear something, do something, or even think something, our energetic body is affected, whether consciously or unconsciously.

Your beliefs, your thoughts, your passions, your perceptions, and even your fears, serve to make an imprint on your soul.

Many have heard the saying *what you believe is what you get*; upon further reflection, one has to admit that this is, indeed, always the case.

Research studies continue to show that if a person believes they are truly sick (and are going to die), they never fare as well as the person who taps into their inner strength, believing that they can recover (and will survive).

This example serves to illustrate the power that one's state of mind can have on their health and well-being.

Living The ED Principles

It is now known that what we think (and what we believe) has a direct impact on our lives, our reality and our health.

Many people live a life of constant stress.

They spend little (if any) time meditating on something other than that which keeps them prisoner to their stress.

Their outlook on life is one that is negative, one that is bleak, one that offers no hope.

As a result, they are more prone to sickness which also means that they will demonstrate the markers of an unhealthy lifestyle; unfortunately, this often transfers to unstable relationships as well.

By comparison, the person who takes time to meditate (reflect, ponder, contemplate, spending time in solitude, becoming more mindful) demonstrates a more positive outlook on life.

They exude better health and look younger; so, too, do they have more positive, stable and fulfilling relationships.

Demonstrating positive beliefs, then, is a key step toward creating a positive and successful life.

As you know, a belief is the way you feel about something. What you may not know is that beliefs are deeply rooted.

Having a belief (a mindset, an assumption, an opinion, an hypothesis, a paradigm) is quite different from believing in something.

Believing in something means trusting that what you want can happen.

Believing in something means knowing that what you want will happen.

When you believe in something so deeply, there is not a single doubt, in your mind, that it will happen because the trust is implicit, complete and without question; unfortunately, however, most of us have been raised to disbelieve, courtesy of the old adage if you can't see it, if you can't feel it, if you can't hear it, then it doesn't exist (meaning, of course, that it's not real).

If people were taught to believe that everything works out, that trusting what we want can, and will, happen, the results would be rather remarkable, would they not?

Do you believe, without a doubt, that you can (and will) have everything that you want?

Do you believe, without a doubt, that you are guided to the right situation at the right time?

Do you believe, without a doubt, that you can get to where you want to be in life?

Do you believe, without a doubt, that there is always a way to achieve your goals, but that you just have to find it?

Believing requires complete trust.

Living The ED Principles

Believing requires taking inspired action (meaning that you are doing your part to find solutions) while continuing to trust in the knowingness that you can (and will) achieve your goals.

Learning to believe requires that you learn to work with both your conscious mind as well as your subconscious mind.

Thereafter, you must practice the art of believing by living your life to the fullest; this is referred to as utilizing your creative potential.

The Zone

The Zone is simply an amazing state of mind, for which there are other colloquial terms, such as to be *in the moment, on a roll, in the groove, on fire, in tune, centered* or *singularly focused*.

To be in the Zone is very much a single-minded immersion.

When I am researching and writing, I find myself in the Zone.

The Zone is a state where your awareness of time almost disappears and you become one with what you are doing.

The Zone is the mental state where we produce our greatest results.

The Japanese call it satori; that magical state where you are completely focused on the task at hand, relaxed and mentally clear.

Living The ED Principles

Energies are contained, channeled, positive, energized and totally aligned with the task at hand; you are focused on nothing but the activity in which you are singularly focused.

In short, there exists both a merger of action and awareness as well as a loss of reflective self-consciousness, and the activity, itself, is one that is intrinsically rewarding; an autotelic experience, if you will.

Doing the things that you love, enjoy and feel passionate about (all of which encompass feeling as well as emotion) enable you to access the Zone.

As you are able to concentrate without distraction, the subconscious taking over from the conscious mind, you are able to access the Zone.

It is also imperative that you are able to figure out which type of environment is most conducive to finding your flow; likewise for what types of activities you can engage in (exercising the body and mind, listening to baroque music, engaging in meditation, listening to Alpha brainwave recordings, using visualization techniques, hypnosis, writing at the right time, finding your best time of day, reading material of a positive and inspirational nature).

Happiness

When one is contented, happiness reigns.

If happiness, then, is an inner, spiritual, experience, how does one go about cultivating contentment?

[1] Elimination of all negative thinking, including judgment of others.

[2] Taking the time to meditate in order to develop a deeper relationship with your authentic self.

[3] Living in total love, acceptance and honor of who you are; stop comparing yourself with others.

[4] Doing what you love and/or loving what you do.

[5] Spending time with the people that make you happy.

[6] Controlling what you can whilst letting go of what you cannot (meaning, cease the worry). This does not mean that you surrender, that you give up; instead. you merely let go of the things that are beyond your control.

Living The ED Principles

[7] Being of service to others and paying it forward; when you do what you can for the betterment of humanity, going out of your way to do something for someone else, everyone emerges the winner.

[8] Living your daily life from a place of gratitude and appreciation.

[9] Savoring the moment as you enjoy the miracle of life whilst living in the now.

[10] Reconnecting with childhood dreams.

[11] Saying thank you.

[12] Smiling at everyone you encounter.

[13] Taking the time to listen.

[14] Forgiving yourself and others.

[15] Learning to exercise emotional detachment, so that nothing (and no one) outside of yourself can influence your thoughts, feelings, emotions, words, actions.

What can you do to invite happiness into your life today?

Living Your Greatness

You are truly great.

The time to *live* your greatness is now.

While your true (authentic) Self is always connected to Source, who you think you are comes from listening to other people (instead of listening to yourself).

Most of us have a tendency to believe what others tell us to believe.

In addition, we come to believe (and think) that what other people think of us is more important than what we think of ourselves.

As long as one lives their life according to these premises, they will never be able to focus on who they really are.

Living your greatness is not about who you are not.

Living The ED Principles

Living your greatness is not about what you cannot do.

Living your greatness is not about what you do not have.

Living your greatness is not about what you cannot accomplish.

Living your greatness is about being who you are.

Living your greatness is about living your life in truth.

Living your greatness is about living your life in alignment with Source.

Living your greatness is about letting life unfold through you.

Living your greatness is about being passionate about what you do.

Living your greatness is about maintaining a high level of expectation.

Living The ED Principles

Living your greatness is about letting go and trusting the creation process.

Living your greatness is about acknowledging that you are the master of your own reality.

Living your greatness is about knowing that things will continue to work out in your favor, even if the outcome is something that you did not expect.

To live your greatness, you must *know who you are*.

To live your greatness, you must embrace the moment for this is the key to experiencing gratitude.

You are the Legacy that you leave behind.

In Summation

As stated at the very beginning of this book, the ED Principles are comprised of two key components; namely, [1] I <u>expect</u> the best, and [2] I <u>deserve</u> the best.

According to John Harricharan, award winning author of <u>When You Can Walk On Water, Take The Boat</u> ... *becoming successful is not about struggles or working hard or reading how-to manuals. Being successful is really dependent on a number of factors that could be managed and directed by each and everyone of us. Success is not even about abilities nor about talents, but about such seemingly abstract things as* beliefs, self-esteem, inspiration, choice, gratitude *and the like. Work on those things and success, in any sense of the word, will become a surety.*

I have done my best, within these pages, to introduce you, the reader, to a variety of reflective topics so that you, too, can learn to expect the best, whilst also knowing, and believing wholeheartedly, that you truly deserve the best.

John also states that *knowing what is happening around you is not nearly as important as what* you think *is happening around you. In other words, what is happening* inside *you is much more important than what is happening around you.*

In accordance with this, being successful is all about having a certain mindset, if you will, meaning that being happy, prosperous and successful are *choices that we make*.

You were born to live a life filled with love, desire, passion and happiness; a life through which to express your unique talents.

You were born to live a life of prosperity, peace of mind and creativity.

You were born to live a life of truth, honesty and integrity.

You are meant to do *great* things.

Living The ED Principles

There is only one person that you have the power to change; that person is yourself.

You are here to live *your* life. The time for change is now!

http://consciousresonance.net/?p=2206

Living The ED Principles

In the astute words of Panache Desai ...[61] *the key to changing the world, to changing your life, and to empowering those around you is authenticity: the willingness to be yourself, the willingness to be vulnerable, the willingness to feel, the willingness to live.*

In continuation, Panache also states that *I am simply reminding you of who you truly are, supporting you into self-love and acceptance by eradicating the judgment that you have imposed on yourself and society has opposed on you.*

I hope that this tome, in some way, also serves to do the same.

Change Your Energy, Change Your Life [62]

---

[61] http://www.panachedesai.com/
[62] http://www.panachedesai.com/oprah-and-panache-success

Further Acknowledgement

Life does not hold anything back from us; in retrospect, we hold ourselves back from life, mainly because we believe that we are separate from our inherent goodness, from each other, from the Source of All That Is, from infinity.

In truth, we embody infinity for we are unique individuated aspects of the One.

We embody the power, the presence, the love, the wisdom, the genius, the joy and the inexhaustible supply of wealth and abundance of life itself.

We are here to wake up to this very truth, this feeling in our heart that says I am ready, willing and able; in my intent, I *can* and I *am*.

If this truth is not active in your consciousness, it cannot be in your experience.

Living The ED Principles

Everything that comes into your life is an activity of your consciousness.

Take the time to acknowledge, take the time to give thanks, take the time to celebrate, the fact that everything that comes into your life is coming from your consciousness, for you *are* the Creator that you seek.

You also need to acknowledge the only thing that the world provides ... feedback.

The outer world is the mirror reflection of the inner world.

As long as you like what you see, continue to carry on.

If you do not like what you see, know that only you can change the reflection.

You are responsible for everything else because all that you experience is emanating from your consciousness; this, then, becomes what you must continue build upon.

Living The ED Principles

The more you appreciate what it is that you have created (joy, peace, love, beauty, abundance, expansiveness, freedom, fulfillment, bliss), the more it grows and expands.

Consciousness is the source of all power and supply.

Likewise, in the giving of your time (your talent, your gift, your knowledge) without conditions, you begin to feel a sense of abundance emanating from within.

Focus on the vision of you living your life at its utmost, through being, doing, having, contributing and creating in a way that stirs your soul to song and excites you.

The world is the canvas upon which you have come here to paint your masterpiece.

The world is the stage upon which you have come to enact a divine production.

You are also here to keep yourself awake to this truth.

Living The ED Principles

As you continue to awaken, living through your individual example, you demonstrate what is possible so that others may seek out the same.

Quantum Physics states that as you are transforming yourself, you also expanding the whole collective, uplifting all of human consciousness; so, too, is this the opportunity that stands before you.

You merely have to reach out and take hold.

You are as the clay, completely receptive and responsive to all modes of emotional expression.

So, too, are you the potter of your soul.

Buddhist Prayer of Forgiveness

If I have harmed anyone in any way, either knowingly or unknowingly through my own confusions, I ask their forgiveness.

If anyone has harmed me in any way, either knowingly or unknowingly through their own confusions, I forgive them.

And if there is a situation I am not yet ready to forgive, I forgive myself for that.

For all the ways that I harm myself, negate, doubt, belittle myself, judge or be unkind to myself through my own confusions, I forgive myself.

You are here to liberate your life.

Bibliography

All of the transformational tools and websites listed herein have been utilized by the author whilst on her spiritual journey of learning to live these ED principles.

AFFIRMATIONS

5 Bedtime Affirmations [63]

8 Morning Affirmations [64]

Affirm-A-Life Master Class [65]

Daily Affirmations [66]

---

[63] http://www.prolificliving.com/blog/2013/10/10/bedtime-affirmations-for-sleep/
[64] http://www.prolificliving.com/blog/2013/07/15/morning-affirmations-before-getting-out-of-bed/
[65] http://www.goalzila.com/affirmalife/
[66] http://www.healyourlife.com/affirmations

Free Affirmations [67]

How Positive Affirmations Changed My Life [68]

How to Use Affirmations Effectively [69]

The Only 100 Positive Affirmations That You Will Ever Need [70]

Using Affirmations [71]

Vital Affirmations for Your Life [72]

AFORMATIONS

Aformation Recordings [73]

---

[67] http://www.freeaffirmations.org/
[68] http://www.freeaffirmations.org/how-positive-affirmations-changed-my-life?utm_source=My-Story&utm_medium=email&utm_campaign=Autoresponder
[69] http://www.wikihow.com/Use-Affirmations-Effectively
[70] http://www.prolificliving.com/blog/2012/08/27/100-positive-affirmations/
[71] http://www.mindtools.com/pages/article/affirmations.htm
[72] http://www.vitalaffirmations.com/
[73] http://www.iafform.com/index.php

iAfform Audio Series (Noah St. John) [74]

Noah St. John: The Abundant Lifestyle Authority [75]

Tap on Afformations for Success [76]

The Afformations Blueprint: A Step-By-Step Formula To Design The Life Of Your Dreams (Noah St. John) [77]

BINAURAL BEATS TECHNOLOGY

It is important to denote that binaural beats only work with headphones.

Enhanced Learning and Focus Level 1 (Pat O'Bryan) [78]

---

[74] http://noahstjohn.com/products/iafform-audio-afformations/
[75] http://afformations.com/try-afformations/?utm_expid=71346862-31&utm_referrer=http%3A%2F%2Fnoahstjohn.com%2F
[76] http://eftfixeseverything.blogspot.ca/2011/03/new-faster-way-to-calm-down-and.html
[77] http://www.afformations.com/letter/
[78] http://instantchange.com/level1/

Living The ED Principles

Enhanced Learning and Focus Level 2 (Pat O'Bryan) [79]

What are Binaural Beats? [80]

BRAINWAVE ENTRAINMENT

Brainwave College [81]

<u>Harmonic Ascension: Frequency Is Everything</u> (Jody Sachse) [82] is one of my favorite places to visit.

<u>Life Response Frequencies</u> (Jeffrey Gignac) [83]

<u>Mystic Mindpower</u> (Jody Sachse) [84]

Scientists and quantum physicists have told us that everything is made up of energy.

We know that energy can be measured as a frequency; in fact, everything around us exists at a certain frequency.

---

[79] http://instantchange.com/level2/
[80] http://www.binauralbeatsmeditation.com/the-science/
[81] http://www.brainwavecollege.com/
[82] http://harmonicascension.com/
[83] http://jeffreygignac.com/life-response-frequencies/
[84] http://mysticmindpower.com/

Light has a frequency, smells have a frequency and thoughts have a frequency.

We all have thought patterns, in different brainwave states, all of which can be measured in frequency.

In short, frequency makes up everything we can see and everything we cannot see.

If you can change a certain frequency, you can change everything.

While our mental state affects our brainwaves, the opposite is also true, meaning that *our brainwaves affect our mental state*. This means that we can actually control our mental state by controlling our brainwaves, which is the power that exists behind Brainwave Entrainment.

[Mystic Mindpower Evolution Brainwave Entrainment Meditation Guide](http://mysticmindpower.com/mp3/MME-Guide.pdf) [85]

---

[85] http://mysticmindpower.com/mp3/MME-Guide.pdf

Living The ED Principles

CONSCIOUSNESS ELEVATION

Alchemy Radio [86]

Fukushima: From Why to How [87]

Fukushima News [88]

Ida Lawrence's Blog [89]

Life is Easy [90]

Mindvalley Academy Blog [91]

Natural News [92]

Waking Times [93]

---

[86] http://alchemyradio.podomatic.com/
[87] http://talk2momz.com/2013/11/05/fukushima-from-why-to-how/
[88] http://www.naturalnews.com/Fukushima.html
[89] http://talk2momz.com/
[90] http://lifeiseasybook.com/
[91] http://blog.mindvalleyacademy.com/
[92] http://www.naturalnews.com/index.html
[93] http://www.wakingtimes.com/

ENERGY VAMPIRES

2 Steps to Feeling More Confident Around Emotional Vampires [94]

5 Signs of an Energy Vampire [95]

10 Tips to Protect Yourself from Energy Vampires [96]

Energy Vampires and How to Survive Them [97]

Energy Vampires: A New Name for an Old Phenomenon [98]

Energy Vampires Steal Your Life Force [99]

---

[94] http://www.astraldynamics.com/psychic-self-defense/feeling-confident-emotional-vampires.php
[95] http://www.hawaiihealings.com/2013/07/5-signs-of-energy-vampire.html
[96] http://trueshiningself.com/10-tips-to-protect-yourself-from-energy-vampires/
[97] http://www.kindredspirit.co.uk/articles/energy-vampires-and-how-to-survive-them/
[98] http://www.messagetoeagle.com/energyvampiresoldphenomena.php#.Uo4LDFy9x9A
[99] http://ufodigest.com/energyvampire.html

Energy Vampires: They Are All Around Us [100]

How to Deal With Energy Vampires [101] [102]

Psychic Energy Vampires [103]

Psychic Vampires and the Use of Etheric Energy [104]

Psychic Vampires and How to Deal With Them [105]

Psychic Vampirism [106]

EFT TAPPING

Discover the Art of EFT [107]

---

[100] http://www.messagetoeagle.com/energyvampires.php
[101] http://www.deliberatereceiving.com/how-to-deal-with-energy-vampires.html#axzz2kwmG6ep1
[102] http://personalexcellence.co/blog/dealing-with-energy-vampires/
[103] http://www.narcissismfree.com/psychic-energy-vampires.php
[104] http://www.themindunleashed.org/2013/06/psychic-vampires-and-use-of-etheric.html
[105] http://www.whitedragon.org.uk/articles/vampyres.htm
[106] http://psychicvampirism.com/
[107] http://www.eftfree.net/

Living The ED Principles

EFT Manual (Sixth Edition) by Gary Craig [108]

Emotional Freedom Technique [109]

Emotional Freedom Technique (EFT) Can Help Reduce Your Stress [110]

Emotional Freedom Technique for Pain Relief [111]

Emotional Freedom Techniques [112]

Learn EFT Tapping [113]

---

[108] http://veteransinfo.tripod.com/eftmanual.pdf
[109] http://eft.mercola.com/
[110] http://articles.mercola.com/sites/articles/archive/2013/04/25/eft-relieves-stress.aspx
[111] http://articles.mercola.com/sites/articles/archive/2012/07/21/eft-for-pain-relief.aspx
[112] http://www.eftuniverse.com/
[113] http://www.thrivingnow.com/tapping/

Living The ED Principles

Tapping in Your Positive Feelings [114]

Tapping for Stress Relief CD (free download) [115]

The Gold Standard for EFT [116]

The Tapping Solution (Nick and Jessica Ortner) [117]

GUIDED MEDITATION

Audio Dharma: Guided Meditations [118]

Guided Mind [119]

Meditation Oasis [120]

---

[114] http://articles.mercola.com/sites/articles/archive/2006/06/08/tapping-in-your-positive-feelings.aspx
[115] http://www.thetappingsolution.com/blog/eft-stress-relief-audios/
[116] http://www.emofree.com/
[117] http://www.thetappingsolution.com/
[118] http://www.audiodharma.org/series/1/talk/1835/
[119] https://www.guidedmind.com/
[120] http://www.meditationoasis.com/

Self-Realization Fellowship: Guided Meditations [121]

The Art of Living: Online Guided Meditation [122]

The Chopra Center: Guided Meditations [123]

The Guided Meditation Site [124]

The Mirror of Mindfulness (Sam Harris) [125]

UCLA Mindful Awareness Research Center [126]

HO'OPONOPONO

History of Ho'oponopono [127]

---

[121] http://www.yogananda-srf.org/Guided_Meditations.aspx#.UlW-7lznh9A
[122] http://www.artofliving.org/online-guided-meditation
[123] http://www.chopra.com/community/online-library/guided-meditations
[124] http://www.the-guided-meditation-site.com/what-is-guided-meditation.html
[125] http://www.samharris.org/blog/item/mindfulness-meditation
[126] http://marc.ucla.edu/body.cfm?id=22
[127] http://soultransync.com/history-of-hooponopono/

Living The ED Principles

Ho'oponopono [128]

Ho'oponopono Help [129]

Ho'oponopono Insights Blog (Saul Maraney) [130]

Prayers of Morrnah Simeona [131]

Return To Zero Point: Ho'oponopono For A Better Life And A Joyful Reality (Robert F. Ray) [132]

The Foundation of I [133]

There Is A Way [134]

---

[128] http://www.lomilomi-massage.org/hooponopono.html
[129] http://hooponoponohelp.com/
[130] http://hooponoponoinsights.wordpress.com/
[131] http://www.mediafire.com/download/vk7tle2l94dc6zi/Prayers+of+Morrnah+Simeona.pdf
[132] http://returntozeropoint.com/
[133] http://www.hooponopono.org/
[134] http://www.thereisaway.org/Ho'oponopono_cleaning_meditation.htm

Zero Limits (Joe Vitale) [135]

Z Plus Advanced Ho'oponopono Subliminal Clearing [136]

HYPNOSIS

Hypnosis Live [137] is a website where you will find 200 self-hypnosis MP3 audio downloads, all created by qualified hypnosis professionals.

Mindfit Hypnosis [138] is a website that offers hypnosis (hypnotherapy) sessions based on a wide variety of topic areas. They also offer a FREE online hypnotic induction video. [139]

Natural Hypnosis [140] is a website whereby you will find CDs and MP3s that can be used to help you change your life.

---

[135] http://www.zerolimits.info/
[136] http://www.subliminalclearing.com/
[137] http://www.hypnosislive.com/
[138] http://www.mindfithypnosis.com/all-hypnosis-mp3
[139] http://www.mindfithypnosis.com/free-online-hypnosis-induction
[140] http://www.naturalhypnosis.com/

Living The ED Principles

They also offer three FREE albums so that you can see if hypnosis is right for you. [141] I find the voice of Brennan Smith to be very soothing.

LIFE FORCE ENERGY

9 Ways to Enhance Your Life Force Energy [142]

A Complete Guide to Understanding and Working with Life Force Energy [143]

The Chakra System [144]

LIFESTYLE CHANGES

Beginner Plan: Lifestyle Changes [145]

---

[141] http://www.naturalhypnosis.com/l/try-hypnosis-free/
[142] http://cowabungalife.com/2013/11/02/affirmations/
[143] http://www.thehealersjournal.com/2013/04/26/working-with-life-force-energy/
[144] http://www.expressionsofspirit.com/yoga/chakras.htm
[145] http://www.mercola.com/nutritionplan/beginner_lifestyle_changes.htm

Living The ED Principles

Intermediate Plan: Lifestyle Changes [146]

Advanced Plan: Lifestyle Changes [147]

John Harricharan's 12 Power Principles [148]

Master Your Inner Game [149]

LISTEN TO YOUR INTUITION

Infinity Program [150]

LIVE FEARLESSLY

The Pathless Path [151]

---

[146] http://www.mercola.com/nutritionplan/intermediate_lifestyle_changes.htm

[147] http://www.mercola.com/nutritionplan/advanced_lifestyle_changes.htm

[148] http://www.12powerprinciples.com/

[149] http://dranthony.com/recommends/drainterviewlsc.html

[150] http://www.immrama.org/infinity/infinity-program-boost-your-intuition.html

[151] http://www.phoenixcentre.com/blog/2007/10/30/live-fearlessly-7-tips/

MANIFESTATION

Creating a Better Life (Carol Tuttle) [152]

Emergineering Mastery [153]

Make Your Mind A Money Magnet video (Dr. Robert Anthony) [154]

Manifest A Miracle (Gary Evans) [155]

Napoleon Hill's Most Controversial Technique (Quantum Jumping) [156]

---

[152] https://ct.liveyourtruth.com/store/ct/all-products-carol-tuttle
[153] http://derekrydall.com/main/emergineering-mastery/
[154] http://www.thesecretofdeliberatecreation.com/moneymagnetspecial.html
[155] http://www.manifestmiracle.com/
[156] http://www.stealthesesecretsyet.com/napoleon-hills-most-controversial-technique/

Living The ED Principles

Practical Reflections on How to Successfully Manifest Things in Your Life [157]

The 7 Essential Universal Laws (Christy Whitman) [158]

The 11 Forgotten Laws (Bob Proctor, Mary Morrissey) [159]

The Hidden Secret in Think and Grow Rich (Brian Kim) [160]

The New Message of a Master (Kristen Howe) [161]

Unlock the Power of Now (Kristen Howe) [162]

Vibration Radiation (Derek Rydall) [163]

---

[157] http://articles.mercola.com/sites/articles/archive/2006/06/24/practical-reflections-on-how-to-successfully-manifest-things-in-your-life.aspx
[158] http://www.7essentiallaws.com/essentiallaws.php
[159] http://www.the11forgottenlaws.com/
[160] http://www.briankim.net/hiddensecret.php
[161] http://www.newmessageofamaster.com/
[162] http://www.unlockthepowerofnow.com/
[163] http://derekrydall.com/vibrationradiation/

Living The ED Principles

Wealth Meditation Manifestation Audio [164]

MEDITATION

How Meditation Changes Your Brain [165]

How to Meditate (Sam Harris) [166]

Meditation in Motion (Tai Chi) [167]

Meditation Lowers Your Blood Pressure and Protects Your Heart [168]

---

[164] http://www.secretsofmeditation.com/blog/guided/wealth-manifesting/

[165] http://articles.mercola.com/sites/articles/archive/2008/07/12/how-meditation-changes-your-brain.aspx

[166] http://www.samharris.org/blog/item/how-to-meditate

[167] http://fitness.mercola.com/sites/fitness/archive/2011/02/26/for-health-benefits-try-tai-chi.aspx

[168] http://articles.mercola.com/sites/articles/archive/2010/01/09/try-meditation-to-lower-your-blood-pressure-and-protect-your-heart.aspx

Living The ED Principles

Meditation Made Easy [169]

Meditation MP3s [170]

Meditation's Real Effects on Health [171]

The Meditation Podcast [172]

What is Transcendental Meditation? [173]

MINDFULNESS

Abundance and Happiness [174]

---

[169] http://personal-growth-project.com/ten-minutes-to-a-better-mind-meditation
[170] http://thirdeyeactivation.com/downloads/
[171] http://articles.mercola.com/sites/articles/archive/2003/09/20/meditation-health.aspx
[172] http://www.themeditationpodcast.com/
[173] http://articles.mercola.com/sites/articles/archive/2013/01/12/meditation-benefits.aspx
[174] http://www.abundance-and-happiness.com/

Living The ED Principles

Being At Ease in Your Life Mindfulness Meditation Audio [175]

How to Enjoy What You Are Doing, No Matter What [176]

Improve Your Focus and Cognitive Function with Mindfulness [177]

The Abundance Prayer [178]

The Law of Resonance [179] [180]

---

[175] http://www.mindbodytrainingcommunity.com/2013/09/09/mini-meditation-being-at-ease-in-the-midst-of-it-all/

[176] http://articles.mercola.com/sites/articles/archive/2007/11/15/how-to-enjoy-what-you-are-doing-no-matter-what.aspx

[177] http://articles.mercola.com/sites/articles/archive/2013/04/13/mindfulness.aspx

[178] http://www.stealthesesecretsyet.com/abundance-prayer-the-most-powerful-prayer-ive-ever-used/

[179] http://www.youtube.com/watch?v=cAZ-sjywM0s

[180] http://ascensionglossary.com/index.php/Law_of_Resonance

The Law of Resonance, Part 1 [181]

The Law of Resonance, Part 2 [182]

The Law of Resonance, Part 3 [183]

The Law of Resonance, Part 4 [184]

The Law of Resonance, Part 5 [185]

Ocean Mindfulness Meditation Audio [186]

PERSONAL GROWTH

Basic Law of Attraction Practitioner Certification Course [187]

---

[181] http://sivasakti.com/articles/tantra/resonance-art62.html
[182] http://sivasakti.com/articles/tantra/resonance-art63.html
[183] http://sivasakti.com/articles/tantra/resonance-art64.html
[184] http://sivasakti.com/articles/tantra/resonance-art65.html
[185] http://sivasakti.com/articles/tantra/resonance-art66.html
[186] http://www.secretsofmeditation.com/blog/guided/mindfulness-meditation/
[187] http://www.loatraining.com/

Living The ED Principles

Do What You Love [188]

I Never Knew I Had A Choice: Explorations in Personal Growth [189]

Life Coach Practitioner Certification Course [190]

Managing through Change ebook [191]

NLP Practitioner Certification Course [192]

Personal Development Articles [193]

Personal Growth Project [194]

---

[188] http://dowhatyouloveforlife.com/

[189] http://www.usd.ac.id/fakultas/pendidikan/bk/f113/Materi%20Kuliah%20dan%20E-book/I-Never-Knew-I-Had-a-Choice%209th%20edition.pdf

[190] http://www.lifecoachingcertified.com/index.html

[191] http://bookboon.com/en/managing-through-change-ebook

[192] http://www.hypnosiscertified.com/nlp/special-sale.html

[193] http://www.essentiallifeskills.net/personaldevelopmentarticles.html

[194] http://personal-growth-project.com/

Living The ED Principles

What is a Life Coach? [195]

POSITIVE THINKING

6 Minutes to Success [196]

20 Ways to Find, Sustain and Share Happiness [197]

22 Positive Habits of Happy People [198]

Simple Secrets of How to Be Happy [199]

---

[195] http://www.allpsychologycareers.com/career/life-coach.html
[196] http://www.getresultsthatstick.com/
[197] http://articles.mercola.com/sites/articles/archive/2006/01/17/20-ways-to-find-sustain-amd-share-happiness.aspx
[198] http://articles.mercola.com/sites/articles/archive/2013/04/08/22-happy-habits.aspx
[199] http://articles.mercola.com/sites/articles/archive/2008/01/19/simple-secrets-of-how-to-be-happy.aspx

Living The ED Principles

Talk to Oracle [200] has been designed and created to help you master your emotions and give you new insights in how to create new powerful meanings.

Tapping In Your Positive Feelings [201]

The Daily Motivator (Ralph Marston) [202]

The Four Steps to a Super Attitude [203]

Your Confident Self Meditation Audio [204]

---

[200] http://talktooracle.co.uk/

[201] http://articles.mercola.com/sites/articles/archive/2006/06/08/tapping-in-your-positive-feelings.aspx

[202] http://greatday.com/

[203] http://articles.mercola.com/sites/articles/archive/2001/10/24/attitude.aspx

[204] http://www.mindbodytrainingcommunity.com/2013/10/07/discover-your-confident-self/

STRESS

9 Strategies to Stay Emotionally Healthy [205]

10 Simple Steps to Help De-Stress [206]

Cumin Doubles as a Memory Booster and Stress Reliever [207]

Emotional Freedom Technique (EFT) Can Help Reduce Your Stress [208]

---

[205] http://articles.mercola.com/sites/articles/archive/2013/04/25/emotional-health-tips.aspx

[206] http://articles.mercola.com/sites/articles/archive/2012/05/10/10-steps-to-manage-stress.aspx

[207] http://articles.mercola.com/sites/articles/archive/2011/08/17/this-kitchen-spice-doubles-as-a-memory-booster-and-stress-reliever.aspx

[208] http://articles.mercola.com/sites/articles/archive/2013/04/25/eft-relieves-stress.aspx

Healing Depression with Energy Therapy [209]

How Stress Affects Your Heart and Gut Health [210]

How Stress Wreaks Havoc on Your Gut and What to Do About It [211]

More Evidence That Stress and Cancer Are Linked [212]

More Evidence That Stress Is a Major Factor for Infections [213]

---

[209] http://articles.mercola.com/sites/articles/archive/2006/04/13/healing-depression-with-energy-therapy.aspx

[210] http://articles.mercola.com/sites/articles/archive/2013/03/28/stress-affects-heart.aspx

[211] http://articles.mercola.com/sites/articles/archive/2012/04/09/chronic-stress-gut-effects.aspx

[212] http://articles.mercola.com/sites/articles/archive/2006/11/25/more-evidence-stress-and-are-cancer-linked.aspx

[213] http://articles.mercola.com/sites/articles/archive/2003/07/16/stress-infections.aspx

Needle This: Study Hints at How Acupuncture Works to Relieve Stress [214]

Positive Outlook Buffers Damaging Effects of Stress [215]

Rejuvenating Guided Meditation [216]

Stress Linked to Cancer [217]

Stress Symptoms, Signs and Causes [218]

Stress: The New Cause of Alzheimers Disease [219]

---

[214] http://articles.mercola.com/sites/articles/archive/2013/03/30/acupuncture-benefits.aspx

[215] http://articles.mercola.com/sites/articles/archive/2005/04/06/stress-part-eight.aspx

[216] http://www.mindbodytrainingcommunity.com/2013/11/18/rejuvenating-guided-meditation/

[217] http://articles.mercola.com/sites/articles/archive/2010/02/04/stress-linked-to-cancer.aspx

[218] http://www.helpguide.org/mental/stress_signs.htm

[219] http://articles.mercola.com/sites/articles/archive/2013/10/10/

Veggie-Heavy Stress Reduction Regimen Shown to Modify Cell Aging [220]

SUBLIMINAL MESSAGING

Mindfit Hypnosis [221] is a website that offers subliminal message therapy sessions based on a wide variety of topic areas.

They also offer a FREE subliminal session entitled Live Life with Passion and Purpose, [222] something we all need to be reminded of.

---

stress-alzheimers-dis-ease.aspx?e_cid=20131010Z1_PRNL_art_1&utm_source=prmrnl&utm_medium=email&utm_content=art1&utm_campaign=20131010Z1

[220] http://articles.mercola.com/sites/articles/archive/2013/10/07/stress-reduction.aspx

[221] http://www.mindfithypnosis.com/subliminal-mp3

[222] http://www.mindfithypnosis.com/live-with-passion-and-purpose-subliminal-message

Real Subliminal [223] is a website whereby you will find CDs and MP3s that can be used to help you change your life.

Thought Inspire Subliminal Audios [224] use BrainTune® which is a patented technology to change your brainwave states, meaning that the subliminal messages go deeper into your mind (leading to and more permanent results).

SUCCESS CONSCIOUSNESS BOOKS

Affirmations: Words with Power [225]

Emotional Detachment for a Better Life [226]

How to Focus Your Mind [227]

---

[223] http://www.realsubliminal.com/
[224] http://www.thoughtinspire.com/products.html
[225] http://www.successconsciousness.com/books/affirmations_words_power.htm
[226] http://www.successconsciousness.com/books/emotional-detachment-for-better-life.html
[227] http://www.successconsciousness.com/books/how-to-focus-your-mind.html

Living The ED Principles

Peace of Mind in Daily Life [228]

Visualize and Achieve [229]

Willpower and Self-Discipline [230]

THE LAW OF ATTRACTION

It does seem strange to refer to the Law of Attraction as a universal law, especially as many feel that it only seems to work for a lucky few. If you broach the subject with most LOA experts, they instantly change the subject. Joe Vitale, however, takes the time to tackle the subject in a new video entitled The Secret Mirror. Like a great many who were excited about The Secret, while also suspecting that there was still something missing, the watching of this video is a key piece to solving the puzzle. [231]

---

[228] http://www.successconsciousness.com/books/peace-of-mind-in-daily-life.htm
[229] http://www.successconsciousness.com/books/visualize-and-achieve.html
[230] http://www.successconsciousness.com/books/willpower-and-self-discipline.html
[231] http://www.vitalesecrets.com/campaigns/tsm/index.php

Living The ED Principles

Abundant Living through Inspired Action [232]

The Law of Attraction (an inspirational video) [233]

Understanding and Working With the Law of Attraction to Create a Better Life [234]

THE SUBCONSCIOUS MIND

7 Steps to Success Program [235]

75 Ways to Think Your Way into Good Health [236]

---

[232] http://www.lawofattractionkey.com/

[233] http://articles.mercola.com/sites/articles/archive/2010/11/01/the-law-of-attraction-an-inspirational-video.aspx

[234] http://articles.mercola.com/sites/articles/archive/2006/04/27/understanding-and-working-with-the-law-of-attraction-to-create-a-better-life.aspx

[235] http://7steps2success.net/free-stuff

[236] http://articles.mercola.com/sites/articles/archive/2008/07/19/75-ways-to-think-your-way-into-good-health.aspx

Auditory Beats in the Brain (Dr. Gerald Oster) [237]

Expand the Power of Your Mind [238]

How to Communicate with Your Subconscious Mind [239]

How to Predict Your Future: Create It [240]

How Your Thoughts Can Cause of Cure Cancer [241]

If your Conscious Mind wants one thing and your Subconscious Mind wants something else, it is impossible to create what you want; in truth, these counter-intentions work

---

[237] http://www.accrete.com/bwe/BWE_Articles/G%20Oster%20-%20Auditory%20Beats%20in%20the%20Brain.pdf
[238] http://www.balancedview.org/en/expand-the-power-of-your-mind?gclid=CMiqz8LC7rkCFRTxOgodZ34AvQ
[239] http://creativethinking.net/articles/2012/08/18/how-to-communicate-with-your-subconscious-mind/
[240] http://articles.mercola.com/sites/articles/archive/2006/02/28/we-choose-every-thought-we-think-and-we-can-create-any-thought-we-want.aspx
[241] http://articles.mercola.com/sites/articles/archive/2008/02/19/how-your-thoughts-can-cause-or-cure-cancer.aspx

to sabotage your manifestations. Life Lessons [242] is a program that provides powerful, positive weekly lessons that will [1] energetically motivate you to keep moving forward, [2] renew your energy and commitment to your goals, [3] boost your immunity to the negative bombardment faced from individuals and the media, and [4] assist and accelerate your ability to manifest your desires, further enabling you to build a life filled with the financial rewards, respect and loving relationships that you deserve.

Maximize Your Potential through the Power Of Your Subconscious Mind for a More Spiritual Life [243]

Mind Force Secrets: The Power of the Mind (Al Thomas Perhacs) [244]

---

[242] http://dranthony.com/recommends/lifelessons.html
[243] http://www.audible.com/pd/Self-Development/Maximize-Your-Potential-Through-the-Power-of-Your-Subconscious-Mind-for-a-More-Spiritual-Life-Audiobook/B0052YQXIC/
[244] http://mind-force.s3.amazonaws.com/Power-of-the-Mind-2012_MTPOTM.pdf

Living The ED Principles

Mind Power: You Create Your Reality [245]

Quantum Warrior: The Future of the Mind [246]

Rules of the Subconscious Mind [247]

The Power of the Subconscious Mind: How to Use It [248]

The Power of Your Subconscious Mind [249]

Think and Grow Rich Chapter 12 [250]

Your Thinking Becomes Your Reality [251]

---

[245] http://www.learnmindpower.com/
[246] http://learnmindpower.podomatic.com/
[247] http://www.2knowmyself.com/subconscious_mind/subconscious_mind_rules_power
[248] http://www.quantumjumping.com/articles/subconscious/subconscious-mind-power/
[249] http://www.ichoosetoheal.com/downloads/the-power-of-your-subconscious-mind.pdf
[250] http://www.sacred-texts.com/nth/tgr/tgr17.htm
[251] http://articles.mercola.com/sites/articles/archive/2001/11/14/belief-reality.aspx

Living The ED Principles

TRUTH

The Great Tomorrow [252]

We Seek To Serve [253]

VISUALIZATION

8 Minute Manifesting (Carl Harvey) [254] is a collection of 20 MP3 audio files that combine brainwave entrainment, NLP, hypnosis and guided visualization; the single most effective way to get results.

Everyday Visualization System (Carl Harvey) [255]

As a Master Practitioner of NLP, Carl has discovered that the fastest way to generate results involves using visualization combined with NLP; hence, his *five-step formula* systematic system.

---

[252] http://www.nickbunick.com/
[253] http://www.weseektoserve.com/
[254] http://www.portalsofspirit.com/creative-visualization-2/
[255] http://www.portalsofspirit.com/creative-visualization/

Living The ED Principles

This program also includes a collection of 13 guided visualization MP3 audio files, training videos as well as several other powerful audio files.

My Ultimate Success (free guided visualization MP3 audio file created by Carl Harvey) [256]

Revealed: A Simple 3-Step Process for Getting What You Want (Carl Harvey's free 20 minute video presentation on how to manifest) [257]

WE ARE ALL CONNECTED

Foundation for Well-Being [258]

---

[256] http://www.everydayvisualization.com/fe/49990-free-mp3
[257] http://visualize.kajabi.com/sp/23885-3-laws
[258] http://www.foundationforwellbeing.org/

Symphony of Science, [259] a project from John D. Boswell, aims to bring scientific knowledge and philosophy to the public, in a novel way that is intended to bring a meaningful message to listeners, while simultaneously providing an enjoyable musical experience.

Why Life Is More than a Series of Accidents or Random Events [260]

YOGA

5 Yoga Poses You Can Do Every Morning to Improve Your Health [261]

There is a very powerful yoga transformation video on this page that necessitates watching.

---

[259] http://symphonyofscience.com/

[260] http://articles.mercola.com/sites/articles/archive/2009/10/03/Why-Life-is-More-than-a-Series-of-Accidents-or-Random-Events.aspx

[261] http://fitness.mercola.com/sites/fitness/archive/2013/09/20/yoga-morning-exercise.aspx

Affiliate Links

To be an affiliate means to be an agent for that product.

Simply put, when you enroll as an affiliate, you promote (or sell) the product of the site (or company) you are enrolled with. You are given an affiliate link wherein you use that link for promotion of the product. When someone clicks on your affiliate link and buys the product you are promoting, you earn a commission for the product sold.

As an affiliate, I believe in sponsoring the products that I have personally tested. Given my spiritual journey of the past 20+ years, there have been a great many products (as you are about to see) that have served, and are continuing to serve, me well.

Your support in purchasing through these links enables me to empower more people worldwide to live more conscious lives and for that I take the time to thank you.

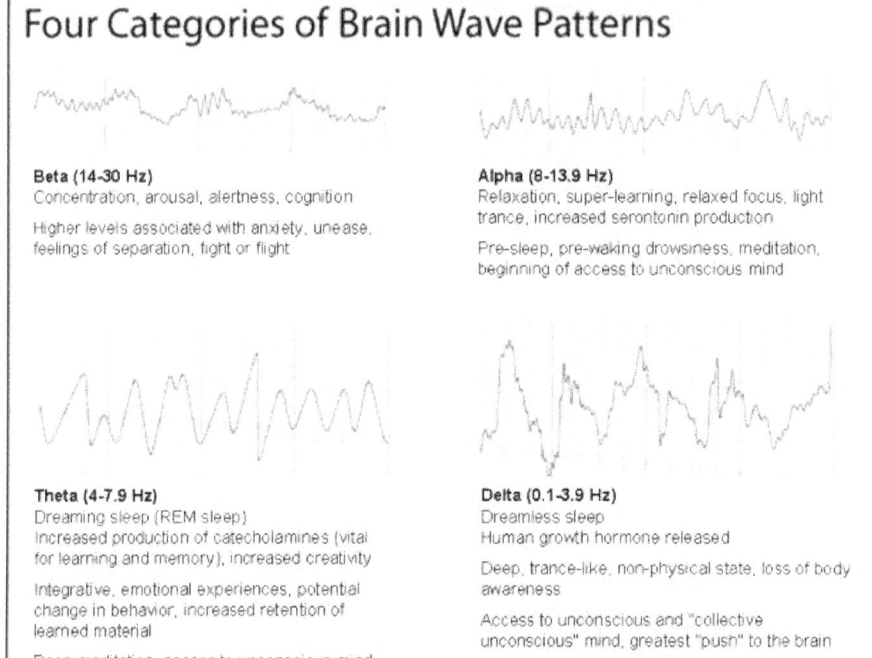

http://www.behappy101.com/images/categories-of-brain-waves.jpg

BRAINWAVE ENTRAINMENT

▶BRAIN SALON (Karl Moore) [262]

The Brain Salon is a scientifically-proven MP3 series that uses specialized sound patterns to change your state of mind.

---

[262] http://www.brainsalon.com/demo/?a=Chebogue

Each of the six audio sessions are designed to bring about a <u>specific</u> state of mind. Just slip on your headphones and get ready for instant results.

▶ BRAINWAVE EVOLUTION SYSTEM (Karl Moore) [263]

The Brain Evolution System (or BrainEv, for short) is a powerful, scientifically-proven 6-level brainwave MP3 program that uses specially created sounds to influence your brainwaves, safely shifting you into a deep state of peak performance, on-demand!

Developed through BrainEv Labs, led by brainwave entrainment pioneer Michael Kelley, the program launch was supported by an investment of over $500,000.

Since then, the Brain Evolution System has become respected as one of the most life-changing programs on the market today; it can help you release stress and tension, sharpen your thinking skills, help you feel happier, rocket your IQ, increase your energy levels and master your

---

[263] http://www.brainev.com/demo/?a=Cheboguc

emotions...all you have to do is listen to one of the brainwave MP3s, for 30 minutes a day.

Sound interesting? Take the time to join us.

▶ GENIUS BRAIN POWER (Cameron Day) [264]

Science has proven that *the human brain is the most complex and powerful computing machine we have ever seen*, but are we really using all that computing power?

The *traditional methods of upgrading your brain* for super-human levels of genius *involve hours of daily meditation* and other disciplines designed to force the brain to adapt to extreme circumstances. Fortunately, science and modern technology have developed a way, courtesy of brainwave entrainment, to impart the peak brain states experienced by seasoned meditators, Buddhist monks, Yogis and top level athletes.

Utilizing computer generated, rhythmically pulsed beats (known as Isochronic beats), *Genius Brain Power* safely,

---

[264] http://b62351w3jinpolf7mrg2cyho26.hop.clickbank.net/

gently and effectively guides your brain to entrain you to your most optimal brainwave frequencies.

▶ INFINITE BRAIN POWER SYSTEM (Todd Lee) [265]

A program unlike any success program you have ever heard of because it works for you on 100% pure auto-pilot!

All you need to do is plug into and listen to our scientifically engineered sessions and let them get to work on re-wiring your brainwaves for success.

Based on a solid foundation of research and development and actual proven and tested results over the last 75 years; founded on work deserving of a Nobel Prize, the information found in the program is totally revolutionary in every way.

▶ NITROFOCUS (Karl Moore) [266]

Discover the scientific solution to increasing your productivity.

---

[265] http://8318e0r2plpjnl9dq0p9pdr5rz.hop.clickbank.net/
[266] http://www.nitrofocus.com/gift/?a=Chebogue

Nitrofocus is a simple MP3 audio program, designed to increase your productivity, by activating your "focus brainwaves."

It works by mixing special brainwave tones, which get your brain into The Zone, with distraction-blocking background sounds.

The result? A simple collection of MP3s (backed by science) that you can listen to while you work, each helping you increase focus and get more done in less time.

▶ SLEEP SALON (Karl Moore) [267]

The Sleep Salon is a brainwave audio program that works by using special tones and pulses, which help influence your brainwave patterns.

Listening to this audio gently takes you down from a waking Alpha state into a deep Delta sleep.

---

[267] http://www.sleepsalon.com/?a=Chebogue

Incredibly powerful and totally safe, the Sleep Salon merely improves on what the brain does naturally, lulling you into a deep sleep within minutes.

Just hit the Play button and listen as you fall asleep. No headphones are required, and you will probably never hear the end of the recording.

The Sleep Salon contains 12 brainwave MP3 sessions. Just read the user guide and listen to the one most suited to the type of insomnia that you are experiencing.

▶ SONIC VITAMINS (Bradley Thompson) [268]

Welcome to Sonic Vitamins, the Web's leading supplier of MP3 brainwave sessions, for significantly changing your mood.

Just slip on your headphones, listen to an MP3 "shot" and watch it change how you feel.

---

[268] http://www.sonicvitamins.com/sonic/?ref=48106

Living The ED Principles

From deep relaxation to faster thinking, increased energy to deep sleep, these scientifically-proven recordings use computer-generated sounds to influence the brainwaves, altering how you feel, in just 30 minutes.

Which Sonic Vitamin pill would you like to take today?

▶ THE MORRY METHOD ™ [269]

A Brainwave Entrainment expert, Morry worked with the Brazilian Government to train officers to reach their peak performance. [270]

All Morry Method™ recordings are mixed to ensure a harmonic balance of sound, science and technology (a combination that provides the maximum effects possible; so, too, do they also follow a strict adherence to comprehensive scientific research.

[1] QUANTUM CONFIDENCE (Morry Zelcovitch) [271]

---

[269] http://www.themorrymethod.com/
[270] http://www.themorrymethod.com/TMMResearch-FIN.3.pdf

Living The ED Principles

When it comes to manifestation, making, and maintaining, the change from a negative state (frustrations, worries, doubts, fears, anxieties) to a positive state (total self confidence, high self esteem) is of utmost importance because until you change the way you think, you will simply continue to manifest more of the same (which is usually what you do not want).

In creating the *Quantum Confidence* system, Morry Zelcovitch has created a responsible, scientific and considerate way to help people identify and deal with what may be holding them back.

Using the *Quantum Confidence* system is very similar to sticking to an exercise regimen or even a proper diet that includes a change in eating habits. Once you get to the point where you want to be, it is important that you keep up a maintenance routine in order to maintain your achieved results.

---

[271] http://c6719bqacevsot5cyw0hx9sbp6.hop.clickbank.net/

The affirmations are designed for each hemisphere of the brain.

So, too, are they designed to be accepted by your mind so that change, real change, may occur in the most efficient and effective way possible.

For those of you who have never used this system (which involves brainwave entrainment), there is something that you should be made aware of.

Brainwave entrainment, when properly engineered, has been shown to allow for the release of deep trauma that has been buried.

Please consider having someone nearby (a professional, a trusted friend, a family member) with whom you can discuss these issues as they arise.

In many cases, repressed emotions and events clear themselves easily, but occasionally they may be difficult.

As people are listening to TMM recording systems, they find that random thoughts continue to pop out of nowhere. Do not fight these thoughts. Simply allow them to be.

It is important to keep remembering that when you resist something, you are engaging in a state of stress.

This program is all about natural states of relaxation, peace and bliss.

[2] QUANTUM MIND POWER (Morry Zelcovitch) [272]

The *Quantum Mind Power* (with TMM) system uses various "sculpted" tones and embedded frequencies in order to get the brain to go into altered (but very natural) states of consciousness.

When the brain reacts to these tones, beneficial neurotransmitters and endorphins are released (which are necessary neuro-chemicals that our brain and body need to function properly, healthfully and naturally).

---

[272] http://cc73e7kzkamouzbh191ptf0te1.hop.clickbank.net/

When the brain is stimulated with pulses, the overall activity of the brain will respond to, and align with, these pulses. By selecting the desired rate, the brain, via the frequency following response (entrainment), can be naturally induced towards the selected brainwave state.

Neural Synergy was specifically designed to help to re-organize the brain to a higher level; allowing it to process more complicated stimuli easier than before.

An integral part of a fitness regimen for the brain, this recording should be listened to once a day.

Eden Energy Wave Dynamics is designed to pump up your energy levels, while silencing the "voices" that tend to make you stagnate and stop moving forward (because they make you think too much, or cause you to fear something).

This recording may be rotated with *Neural Synergy* on alternate days for variety and/or whenever you feel the need for a quick "pick me up."

Living The ED Principles

Whole Brain Gratitude Meditation was designed as a gratitude building meditation. This recording, which is intended to be listened to twice a week, helps you with direction and intent, thereby enabling you to change your current view of the world (which then changes your reality as well). How you look at things and interpret their meaning can be everything, and amazing changes occur when you change how you look at life.

Emotive Brain Wave Hypnosis was designed to help guide you to balance your emotions and experience happiness, allowing you to tap into the deep wiring of your subconscious mind (so that you can better deal with the matters that are most affecting your life). It is intended to be listened to twice a week.

Feel free to sample a 20 minute audio recording. [273]

[3] SPECIALLY PRICED FACEBOOK SPECIALS [274]

---

[273] http://quantum-mind-power-system.com/Gift-for-friends.htm
[274] http://www.themorrymethod.com/tmm.php?id=20

Living The ED Principles

▶ **TRYPNAURAL BRAINWAVE ENTRAINMENT MEDITATION (Niraj Naik)** [275] [276] [277]

Niraj Naik (a musician and scientist with classical training in ancient Indian Vedic and Gregorian music) discovered a strange relationship between music, brainwaves and the harmonic pulse of our planet (the Schumann Resonance).

He recognized that music played with a hypnotic arpeggiated groove at 120bpm and 60bpm would sync perfectly with alpha and theta brainwaves and the Earth's magnetic pulse.

This discovery is what led to the development of this brand new style of brainwave entrainment; a breakthrough meditation technology designed to *stimulate your natural production of tryptamines* (serotonin, melatonin and DMT)so you can benefit from deeper sleep, improved mood, increased mind power, better health, creativity and intuition.

---

[275] http://c6f251lzpkjslwb0s4-ynq3s5r.hop.clickbank.net
[276] http://www.trypnauralmeditation.com/blog/
[277] http://www.trypnauralmeditation.com/subliminal-healing/

Living The ED Principles

As these Trypnaural products feature the beautiful music of amAya (a collaboration between Niraj Naik and Dr Mrigank Mishra, both with an expertise in crafting exquisite sounds and music with a healing touch), their sublime and unique style of music has been gaining incredible popularity, with their music being used in therapy centers, yoga studios and health spas all around the world.[278]

You get access to a frequently updated library of Trypnaural meditation tracks, brainwave entrainment sessions, raw isochronic tones and nature sounds.

You also get special guides that teach you how to create your own subliminal mind programs and guided meditations using free tools that you can find online.

BREATHING

▶ THE POWER OF BREATHING(Bradley Thompson) [279]

---

[278] http://www.amayasounds.com/
[279] http://www.powerofbreathing.com/?ref=48106

Living The ED Principles

For millennia, cultures across the world have known about the magical power of breathing.

Not only does it sustain human life, but it can bring about huge benefits if used correctly.

Backed by years of scientific research, breathwork is one of the simplest, most powerful methods of changing your life (just by changing the way you perform this common human function).

This revolutionary breathwork audio course steadily guides you through a series of expertly-crafted breathing sessions, designed to stimulate the life-changing, healing benefits of breathwork.

Starting with the Level 1 session (8 minutes), you steadily progress to the more powerful breathing patterns in Level 2 (10 minutes), before ultimately advancing to Level 3 (15 minutes).

You will instantly enjoy a feeling of calmness and total mental clarity; many of the deeper benefits will be realized within a couple of weeks.

Enjoy the sessions in the morning, and/or in the evening, whenever you need a mental boost and wish to sharpen your mind.

CHAKRA WORK

▶ALIGNING TO ZERO SUBLIMINAL ALIGNMENT AUDIO [280]

This is a 30 minute downloadable track that is not music; it is a vibrational drone that matches and cycles through your 7 different energy centers (chakras).

Experts agree that aligning our chakras awakens and enhances our consciousness to a higher state of awareness; so, too, do we experience increased relaxation, relief from stress, increased ESP talents, accelerated healing, enhanced imagery, creative breakthroughs, aligned hormones and an instant *in the flow* state.

Our energy centers are challenged on a daily basis; the number one cause of misalignment is stress.

---

[280] http://5c21b-oaegpius4oy0s55q2kcz.hop.clickbank.net/

When your body is in alignment, it can heal itself in ways that modern medicine has been trying to do for hundreds of years.

New research indicates that sound and music both contribute, in a positive way, to our emotional and physical well-being.

Subliminal Alignment harmonically achieves these results in the same way that Tibetan monks have used bowls, bells and overtone chanting for centuries.

▶CHAKRA 7 SYSTEM [281]

This 22 hour training video course is designed to teach you how to reinvigorate and heal your 7 chakras. Carol Tuttle brings together a selection of key modern and traditional healing methods which give you the freedom to uplift and strengthen your chakras in a way that best suits you. Get ready to tap into your chakras and see improvements in every aspect of your life.

---

[281] http://mval.li/?a=3010&c=331&p=r&s1=

CREATIVE VISUALIZATION

BEYOND MANIFESTATION (AN ADVANCED MANIFESTATION SYSTEM) [282]

These audio recordings of the historic seminar go beyond *The Attractor Factor*, *The Power of Intention*, *Ask and It Is Given*, Beyond *Positive Thinking*, The Secret, and virtually every other "How to Manifest" or "Law of Attraction" book, course, or movie out there.

If you want more and are ready for more, you need look no further.

If you are ready to learn how to turbo-charge your ability to manifest, this is it.

If you are ready to go beyond what you know or think you know, here is your chance.

If you are ready to let go of what doesn't work in order to learn (and embrace) that which does, you are there.

---

[282] http://ee3d00m-dmjpgt28wvonhras17.hop.clickbank.net/

If you are open minded, get ready to brace yourself for some powerful goosebumps.

▶ MAKE YOUR VISUALIZATIONS A REALITY (Steve G. Jones) [283]

To put it clearly and succinctly, if you have *not* created a clear and concise vision of how you will achieve financial independence within your mind, then what you have done is created a vision of how you will not achieve it.

In other words, by *not* using visualization to your advantage, you have used it to your disadvantage and perhaps created a vision of yourself working for someone else or just not making the money that you need to be financially free.

Aside from intense training and practice, professional athletes mentally visualize themselves achieving the desired result. This makes it much easier for them to do so in real life situations because the mind cannot tell the difference between an event experienced in real life and a created within the mind.

---

[283] http://c04a7ys3g8rotva7-qrj9vnn6h.hop.clickbank.net/

This, alone, is what makes visualization such a powerful tool.

Clinical hypnotherapist, Steve G. Jones, has been helping people effectively master creative visualization, through the power of hypnosis, for over 25 years.

Taking everything he has learned and discovered, he has created a truly empowering program (that consists of four audio modules, approximately 30 minutes each) to help people master using visualization in the privacy of their own home.

▶MIND MOVIES [284] was denoted the *Best Manifestation Tool for 2007* and after watching the intro video, it was easy to see why.

Whatever the mind can conceive and believe, it can achieve. These truth-filled words were spoken by Napoleon Hill, author of Think and Grow Rich. For people, like me, who have an extremely difficult time with the visualization process, you have finally come to the right place.

---

[284] http://www.mindmovies.com/?10107

If you can create with a joyful and passionate feeling, you are going to accomplish whatever it is that you desire a whole lot faster.

When it comes to visualization, yet another medium, I find it incredibly difficult to see the pictures while also trying to put myself in the image.

It is quite difficult to get emotionally excited about a specific impression when all my mind sees are some dark and fuzzy attempts at a new reality.

Mind Movies allows you to transform a boring vision board into a fun, digital video vision board, one that is filled with positive affirmations, inspiring images and motivating music.

Since having discovered MIND MOVIES, an absolutely phenomenal metaphysical tool, I am finally able to visualize with increasing clarity.

Living The ED Principles

Feel free to watch TIME TO REVOLUTIONIZE [285] as well as AN ABUNDANCE OF BLESSINGS, [286] the two Mind Movies that I was inspired to create.

▶MIND MOVIES MATRIX PROGRAM [287] is an outstanding merger of the original Mind Movies program with the best subconscious programming technology (courtesy of my dear friend, Morry Zelcovitch) that exists, all to bring you the *ultimate experience* in mentally transforming yourself for success.

A Brainwave Entrainment expert, Morry worked with the Brazilian Government to train officers to reach their peak performance. [288]

A program that was two years in the making, all I can say is that this newest version has, by far, totally exceeded *all* of my expectations.

---

[285] http://www.youtube.com/watch?v=UBLFLF4c7cU
[286] http://www.youtube.com/watch?v=rHpH3jBBEBY
[287] http://www.mindmoviesmatrix.com/?10107
[288] http://www.themorrymethod.com/TMMResearch-FIN.3.pdf

Living The ED Principles

▶ QUANTUM JUMPING [289]

Quantum Jumping is an advanced visualization exercise that will enable you to tap into your subconscious mind and discover an infinite number of realities and possibilities.

After spending decades studying meditation, yoga, hypnosis and a variety of other spiritual and metaphysical disciplines, Burt Goldman invented Quantum Jumping in 2008.

Get ready to discover the shocking mind trick (used for centuries by some of the world's most prolific artists, inventors and entrepreneurs) that can help you master any skill, achieve any goal, and live a life of success and fulfillment.

▶ THE MASTER BLUEPRINT(Bradley Thompson) [290]

Considered to be the most powerful wealth building information ever put down in print, countless millionaires

---

[289] http://mval.li/?a=3010&c=463&p=r&s1=
[290] http://www.master-blueprints.com/?ref=48106

Living The ED Principles

from Richard Branson to Anthony Robbins report this book as being the catalyst for their success.

The principles have been proven time and time again, over a period of decades, since 1923, because it reveals to you the "mind map" for success. In other words it contains proven ways of thinking that will enable you to achieve all it is you want to in life: health, wealth, love and happiness are all just a "mind switch" away.

This course trains people the Think And Grow Rich way so that they do not have to attempt to decipher the secrets themselves.

Your life is *a* direct result of decisions and thoughts that you have had and made *in* the past.

Using groundbreaking technology, this course gets you thinking and acting like *the* most successful people *to* ever walk the planet; a way that results *in* dramatic and lasting change *in* your personal and financial life.

This course provides you with a specific action plan, an action plan centred around the book that has created more millionaires than any other ever written, an action plan that can make YOU the next big success story.

▶ THE POWER OF CREATIVE VISUALIZATION WITH LISA NICHOLS [291]

Creative Visualization is a collection of 12 guided meditation audios delivered by Lisa Nichols, based on elements from Shakti Gawain's <u>Creative Visualization</u> and the Silva Method.

Lisa's teachings will take people on an *experiential carpet ride* into their future from a very organic, practical and tangible place of touch, smell, feel and experience.

HEALTH AND WELL-BEING

▶ THE FIVE RITUALS (Bradley Thompson) [292]

Hidden deep inside the Himalayas is a secret *almost* too good to be true. It is a secret that can enable you to look a shocking 30 years younger.

---

[291] http://mval.li/?a=3010&c=961&p=r&s1=
[292] http://www.fiverituals.com/?ref=48106

Living The ED Principles

It is a secret that can remove your wrinkles.

It can restore your natural hair color.

It can improve your memory.

It can correct your eyesight.

It can turbo-charge your energy levels, your strength and your virility.

While this is a strong claim, it is not made lightly.

These are the exact same Five Rituals that were passed onto Peter Kelder, who went on to write <u>The Ancient Fountain of Youth</u> and <u>The Eye of Revelation</u> whereby he documented the amazing power of these five rituals, and how they had the power to radically make anyone look and feel better.

Kelder's work received critical acclaim when it was published in 1939. In just ten minutes a day, you will be seeing results within one week.

HYPNOSIS

▶ **PEAK PERFORMANCE HYPNOSIS (Niraj Naik)** [293]

Fall into a deep sleep in minutes and wake up to peak mental performance, everyday, using the ground breaking Trypnosis Audio Technology, the core of this unique transformational system.

Tell them where to send your free Conscious Mind Trpnosis Primer session (designed to prime your mind for positive change). [294]

LAW OF ATTRACTION

▶ **ATTRACT STUDIO (Bradley Thompson)** [295]

The Law of Attraction works but most people don't get the results, because they are not visualizing the right way.

Visualization is the most important step in the manifestation process.

---

[293] http://f779e6j4e8tnfsfjyd3z0o9y2w.hop.clickbank.net/
[294] http://peakpowerhypnosis.com/
[295] http://www.attractstudio.com/?ref=48106

Living The ED Principles

It focuses your thoughts, keeps your purpose on track, and sends out 'vibrations' that attract those desires into your life.

Many of us who do visualize actually <u>shift our vision</u> along the way by changing what we want.

Others <u>do not add enough emotion</u> to their visualization, leaving the "signal" they send out both limp and lifeless.

Many of us have major problems with the visualization process.

In other words, the vast majority of individuals get nowhere near the powerful results they expect from the Law of Attraction, simply because they are not visualizing the right way.

Why not take the time to create Attraction Movies?

Essentially, they are animated vision boards, incorporating all of your goals and desires.

They use images, videos, music and affirmations, to create an enticing movie, completely customized to your goals.

Attraction Movies are powerful, evoking a wave of; they also consistently highlight your specific goals, without any wavering or change along the way.

Attract Studio is a powerful collection of workbooks, video and audio, that takes you straight to being a Law of Attraction Pro.

▶ DECODING THE ABUNDANCE MINDSET [296]

What are the driving forces that inspire people who excel in every field?

What makes them different, gives them that edge?

What are the secrets to their success?

Do you wonder why you see success all around you, but aren't experiencing it first-hand? It may be because you are unwittingly blocking your successes and sabotaging yourself with doubts, uncertainties, and limiting beliefs on a subconscious level.

---

[296] http://38be0ak4onnfqt86tmwghc5c62.hop.clickbank.net/

Living The ED Principles

To create and attract what you want, your mind must first be convinced of your ability to succeed in all levels of awareness, both *consciously* and *subconsciously*.

This online, multi-media course is designed to help you [1] remove the invisible barriers to your success, [2] unlock your hidden creativity, [3] discover the laws of a successful life, [4] break the cycles of repeating patterns that do not get you what you want, and [5] assist you in manifesting and creating all that you do want.

▶LAW OF ATTRACTION CERTIFICATION PROGRAM [297]

▶LAW OF ATTRACTION WEALTH PRACTITIONER CERTICATION PROGRAM [298]

▶LAW OF ATTRACTION PRO (Bradley Thompson) [299] [300]

---

[297] http://3c4568m5ncnfhl99302dbf1o67.hop.clickbank.net/
[298] http://b904c9x2hesssq0htwo9461673.hop.clickbank.net/
[299] http://www.lawofattractionpro.com/?ref=48106
[300] http://www.lawofattractionpro.com/science.html

You have tried *The Secret*. You have bought manifestation books. You may even have attended a seminar, but you are still *not* getting results with the Law of Attraction.

Bradley Thompson knows why.

In his latest audio course, Bradley distils wisdom from the world's leading Law of Attraction teachers, to bring you the ultimate guide to manifestation success.

▶ LIFE VISION MASTERY [301]

To get going on a better way forward, one thing is for sure: you need to have a vision.

Famous deaf and blind author, Helen Keller, once pointed out that *the most pathetic person in the world is someone who has sight, but has no vision.*

And Steven Covey, in his book <u>The 7 Habits of Highly Effective People</u>, has also recommended, *begin with the end in mind.*

---

[301] http://fl73fzp6iajsgk29yegq83vw0g.hop.clickbank.net/

Put simply, visioning is about how you would like things to be.

It involves having the image of your desired end result as a reference by which you undertake physical actions towards manifesting it.

However, as you will find out later, it is not just any vision that you would want to adopt.

You would want to align with one that connects with your heart, through a higher awareness of who you are.

You also want to learn about how best you can work together with the laws of the Universe so that you can turn your ideal mental picture to reality more easily and effortlessly.

The *Life Vision Mastery Program* is a home-study course that guides you on a heart-centered journey, for the purpose of self-discovery, visioning and bringing your dreams forward.

It is a series of practical journaling-and-visualization exercises that culminates in your making of a vision board.

The *Life Vision Mastery Program* is one that offers you the tools to bring your best life forward.

▶ THE ABSOLUTE SECRET (Bradley Thompson) [302]

There is a single secret that connects a long-lost *Little Red Book* (published in 1926), the world famous software billionaire, Bill Gates, and one very special, well-known, Quantum Physics experiment.

When the student is ready, the teacher will appear.

If you are ready to open your life to success, happiness, joy, wisdom, friendships, unlimited wealth and freedom, this might be something that you want to explore.

▶ THE BELIEF SECRET (Bradley Thompson) [303]

---

[302] http://www.theabsolutesecret.com/?ref=48106
[303] http://www.beliefsecret.com/?ref=48106

Living The ED Principles

In 1948, Claude Bristol published a book that unveiled the *real* secret behind manifestation; BELIEF.

Belief changes both yourself and the world around you. What you expect to happen, very often happens. With belief, your perceptions shift, the world around you changes, and opportunities can become more apparent.

Believe and you can really receive.

▶ THE QUANTUM COOKBOOK(Bradley Thompson) [304]

Having manifested a dream lifestyle over the past 20 years, Bradley Thompson knows the two missing steps that The Secret does not tell you.

He will prove to you that manifesting works brilliantly when you follow his 6 step program. Not only that, but he will hand over $150 if it does not work for you. This just might be something that you also want to check out for yourself.

---

[304] http://www.quantumcookbook.com/?afl=48106

LIFE COACHING

▶LIFE COACHING SECRETS (Bradley Thompson) [305]

MANIFESTATION

▶EMERGINEERING PERSONAL DEVELOPMENT SYSTEM (Derek Rydall) [306]

Whether you are an artist, entrepreneur, writer, teacher, coach, or healer, you can activate your emerging power in every area of your life and actualize more potential than you ever thought possible.

▶ENLIGHTENED BEINGS SUPER MANIFESTOR E-STORE [307]

An e-store that sells manifesting ebooks, affirmation ebooks, guided meditations and a manifesting e-course, all courtesy

---

[305] http://www.life-coaching-secrets.com/?ref=48106
[306] http://www.1shoppingcart.com/app/?Clk=5137396
[307] https://www.enlightenedbeings.com/SM-estore/index.php?r=1&ref=211

of Jafree Ozwald, an absolutely amazing Manifestation Coach.

▶ SOUL PURPOSE BLUEPRINT (Derek Rydall) [308]

You have been taught the exact reverse of how life works.

Bombarded by messages from the moment you were born (you can't do this, you can't be this, what you want is impossible), as a coping mechanism to protect this precious core, you began to close off parts of your authentic, powerful, brilliant, gorgeously outrageous self.

Is it any wonder that you have continued to struggle to know who and what you are and the great purpose you were born for?

Even after becoming aware of what might be possible, is it any wonder why you have had a hard time accepting your potential and really going for it?

---

[308] http://www.1shoppingcart.com/app/?Clk=5137402

Re-connecting to your Soul Purpose Blueprint (that divine DNA) and *bringing your life back into alignment with it* will heal those lifelong traumas, and re-integrate those buried treasures, so that you will never be a victim of circumstances again.

▶ THE LAW OF EMERGENCE (Derek Rydall) [309]

In Derek's words ... *Self-Improvement is an oxymoron. The Self, when truly understood, is already perfect. Just as the acorn contains the oak, the Self has everything it needs to fulfill its higher purpose. When the inner conditions are right, it naturally emerges; bigger, better, and more abundantly than we can imagine. This isn't hyperbole, it's law; the Law of Emergence. Practicing it will enable you to live on the emerging edge, where your greatest potential can unfold in every area of your personal and professional life.*

▶ THE SECRET OF DELIBERATE CREATION (Dr. Robert Anthony) [310]

---

[309] http://www.1shoppingcart.com/app/?af=1559591
[310] http://b514ayx6qnjkjq7n15h-dodod8.hop.clickbank.net/

This program is a dynamite combination of The Da Vinci Code, The Secret and Think and Grow Rich.

Mysterious, suspenseful, and powerfully persuasive, it is now available in a considerably discounted (of over $100) and fully downloadable version.

What Dr. Robert Anthony does in *The Secret of Deliberate Creation* is show you how the natural laws of Quantum Physics, the Law of Attraction, and Cause and Effect can either work for you or against you.

As a conscious and deliberate creator, you, too, will want these laws working for you, 100% of the time.

MEDITATION

▶ CORE ENERGY MEDITATION [311]

---

[311] http://www.mindbodytrainingcompany.com/go.php?Clk=4073087

Scientists have recently made some amazing discoveries about the human bio-energy field and the major energy centers in the body.

These energy centers literally determine how good (or bad) you feel each day.

The better you feel, the more you are able to attract the good things you want into your life.

Kevin Schoeninger (certified holistic fitness trainer, meditation instructor and Reiki Master/Trainer) has developed a 20-minute practice that will balance all your major energy centers.

This is a short daily practice that allows you to balance and energize every aspect of your being; a practice that better enables you to feel healthy and happy (which is all part of your life purpose).

Kevin's *Core Energy Meditation* system also gives you a blueprint for tapping into your personal guidance system. When you feel connected to Source, you know when you are taking the right action for your life in the here and now.

▶ ENNORA BINAURAL BEATS [312]

Ennora Binaural Beats are special meditation music recordings that entrain your brain for better health and well-being, helping to reduce stress and anxiety, increase focus and productivity, improve sleep, heighten spiritual consciousness and more.

Simply listen through headphones and relax; it's that easy.

▶ OMHARMONICS [313]

OmHarmonics is a revolutionary audio meditation product designed and developed after a year of devoted attention by Mindvalley and a team of world-class consciousness engineers.

Powered with binaural beats, heartbeat synchronization and ambient sounds, *OmHarmonics* stimulates your senses in a positive way and is scientifically proven to eliminate

---

[312] http://dbbbdbicghmmft150bwmmocke4.hop.clickbank.net/
[313] http://mval.li/?a=3010&c=563&p=r&s1=

internal and external resistance to allow you to reach an optimal meditative zone in a matter of minutes.

▶THE SECRETS OF MEDITATION, HEALTH AND MANIFESTATION [314] is a comprehensive introduction to meditation, breathing, energy work and manifestation.

What many do not realize is that there are meditation and breathing exercises you can use to reduce stress as well as improve your health, thereby increasing your level of energy and enjoyment of life.

These secrets are simple and yet tremendously powerful. Doing these exercises on a daily basis, as simple as they are, will change your life.

These secrets include how to [1] develop control over your own mind and body, [2] supercharge your energy level and feel great on a day-to-day basis, and [3] work with the

---

[314] http://www.mindbodytrainingcompany.com/go.php?Clk=4073086

Living The ED Principles

power of your subconscious mind to move you toward what would truly fulfill you in your life.

Matt Clarkson has created a complimentary course to help you get started. With each installment, you will get an exercise, inspirational message or tip, to help you calm the mind and reduce stress.

This is an ideal program for anyone with an interest in meditation, self-growth and personal development, as well as for anyone suffering from stress, anxiety or depression.

▶ SPIRITED MEDITATION (Steve G. Jones) [315]

The positive effects of spiritual mediation have been known for thousands of years.

People from all over the worlds have used spiritual mediation to attain a higher degree of enlightenment since the beginning of time.

Some people however, find it difficult to meditate.

---

[315] http://56e464u8lnlspx8kyb1bzgqa8c.hop.clickbank.net/

With so many thoughts running wild within our minds, clearing the mind and achieving the state of pure consciousness can be quite a task.

Achieving the state of pure consciousness in spiritual mediation involves much of the same things that are involved in hypnosis.

The problem was that for many years, getting people to achieve the Alpha state was something that could only be done during a private session at outrageous cost.

Determined to find a better solution, world renowned hypnotist, Steve G. Jones, found a way to create a program that people could use to master the art of spiritual meditation and provide an overall benefit to their life wherever and whenever they wanted.

▶ THE POWER OF PRACTICE [316]

---

[316] http://www.mindbodytrainingcompany.com/go.php?Clk=4073090

Living The ED Principles

If you have had any kind of trouble making The Law of Attraction work in your life, you may be missing one key ingredient, as is shared by Mind-Body Training expert Kevin Schoeninger.

This is the program wherein you will discover the one word never mentioned in The Secret, a concept that is crucial for your happiness and success with the Law of Attraction.

Kevin calls this the Master Tool as used by Oprah, Donald Trump, and all of the great spiritual masters that live their soul's purpose, while also manifesting spectacular results.

▶ THE MEDITATION PROGRAM (Bradley Thompson) [317]

Your brain operates at certain frequencies, depending on what it is doing.

When you are sleeping, you are experiencing Delta. Right now, as you are reading this text, you are in Beta. When you begin meditating, you start delving into lower Alpha.

---

[317] http://www.meditationprogram.com/?rcf=48106

Living The ED Principles

After you have been meditating for years, you start to be able to reach newer, more powerful depths – levels of deep Alpha, deep Theta, and even upper Delta (the levels where you begin to experience profound benefits).

There *is* a way to achieve these depths without having to commit years of your life to daily meditation.

By using binaural beats, a technique discovered in 1839 by German research scientist, Heinrich Wilhelm Dove.

During the process of playing slightly different frequencies into the left and right ear, a third frequency (binaural beat) is generated; the brain automatically follows this frequency, putting you into that very state of mind.

This means that by listening to deep Alpha, deep Theta and upper Delta frequencies, you will be able to quickly replicate states of deep meditation.

Through the process of meditation, you expand the threshold of your mind, thereby giving it more "space" to operate, and automatically releasing negative self-sabotaging habits along the way.

Living The ED Principles

This Meditation Program includes a series of levels, each designed to take you deeper and deeper, expanding the threshold of your mind, bringing you a greater sense of peace and understanding with each session.

Consisting of eight brilliantly-composed levels, each taking you deeper that the last, each level is designed to be listened to for at least a week, at which point you move onto the next.

Levels 1 to 4 begin expanding the threshold of your mind, gradually exploring the deepest states of Alpha.

Levels 5 to 7 cover deep Theta and early Delta.

Level 8 expands your mind into the mid-Delta stage. When you reach this frequency (of about 2.5 Hz), you will be experiencing the most powerful meditation available, something that typically takes years to achieve.

Rather than simply containing the sounds of rain, like most competing products, each level in *The Meditation Program* contains a unique, deep and powerful soundtrack compiled by industry-leading composer, M. Anton. [318]

Meditation is changing; the Meditation Program is where you need to be.

MIND POWER

▶ SUPER MIND EVOLUTION SYSTEM [319]

Since Einstein has proven that energy and mass are interchangeable, various universities and laboratories have been able to either measure or calculate the force generated by a human mind (as in psychokinetic experiments). The obvious conclusion here is that, as mass and energy are interchangeable, the energy generated by human consciousness can be converted into its mass equivalent, the format of which is controlled and directed by the most

---

[318] http://cdn.selfdevelopment.net/meditationprogram.com/mp3/sample.mp3

[319] http://www.supermindevolutionsystem.com/store/?12737

extraordinary of higher-consciousness processes; namely, visualization.

When a human mind clearly, and continually, visualizes an end result, with deep emotion and concentrated intent, then the formatted energy generated is converted into its mass equivalent (meaning the desired result).

Jim Francis, a serious researcher, has a background in both hypnosis and electronic design. The founder of the Australasian Lateral Thinking Newsletter, he has been its editor for the past twelve years.

Having undertaken training in various forms of remote viewing, Jim shows how this medium technique can easily be learned.

Apart from Jim's description of his minddiscoveries and their application, he also points to theserious science that supports his concepts, describing how individuals can take advantage of these scientific suppositions, thereby moving towards a better understanding of how the intuitive mind works.

Living The ED Principles

The substantiated research of Jim Francis, over the course of the last 10 years, was combined with the latest *cutting edge* brain audio technology. As a result, the *Super Mind Evolution System* was born.

The entire system is available in 21 PDF reports and 20 audio mp3 files, all accessible via instant download.

▶REVOLUTIONIZ: HARNESS THE HIDDEN LAWS OF THE UNIVERSE [320]

If you have struggled to understand *exactly* how the Law of Attraction brings abundance and prosperity into your life, all it requires is a relatively small shift in your understanding of how life works.

You may have read all the books on the subject and watched movies like *The Secret* and many others and *still* do not understand the fine intricacies of these universal mechanisms, much less how you can steer them.

---

[320] http://0bc880v9fniijw0mwf56v8kk97.hop.clickbank.net/

Living The ED Principles

In lacking full understanding (because you might be overwhelmed by the barrage of half-truths and myths that prevail), the way you are subconsciously interacting with the universe might actually be bringing you more of the very things you do not want.

Once you learn, once you realize and appreciate the power of understanding the Universal Principles of Life in the way you are about to learn them, courtesy of this program, you can and will draw all the love, money, success, health and happiness you have been longing for directly into your life.

▶ THE UNDISCOVERED PARALLEL, PART 1 [321]

Discover *The Undiscovered Parallel Part 1* which will show you one simple trick to supercharge all techniques used for focusing your mind (as in visualization, affirmations, subliminals, hypnosis, EFT, the Sedona Method, meditation, brainwave entrainment, counseling or therapy) as part of your self-growth journey.

---

[321]

http://www.mindbodytrainingcompany.com/go.php?Clk=40 85676

NLP (NEURO LINGUISTIC PROGRAMMING)

▶THE ULTIMATE NLP COURSE (Bradley Thompson)[322]

NLP (Neuro Linguistic Programming) was co-created by Dr. John Grinder and Dr. Richard Bandler.

Powerful and completely safe, NLP contains so much theory that most people never really get started; the books are too thick and the Advanced Master Practitioner courses can take *months* to complete.

Having crammed years of NLP training down to an awesome new two hour course, we want to show you the techniques that really work and produce amazing results.

For the first time ever, Certified NLP Practitioner Christine Golden has crystallized her years of NLP knowledge into the most dynamic NLP training course available today.

No waiting.

---

[322] http://www.ultimatenlp.com/?ref=48106

Living The ED Principles

No confusion.

No trying to decipher instructions from a guidebook.

Just sit back, listen, and witness the change for yourself.

▶ THE NLP SECRET (Bradley Thompson) [323]

NLP one of the most powerful methods of changing your thoughts in the quickest time possible.

Often used as an alternative to psychotherapy, it works by talking to your brain in its own "language" and altering how you think about things.

To begin, you find a negative pattern that happens automatically in your life (or in the life of your client, if you are a therapist). Negative patterns include feelings such as shyness, fear, stress, procrastination, anger and feeling stuck.

Once you have identified the problem, you simply perform a little trick (that takes about 10 minutes) involving the body.

---

[323] http://www.nlpsecret.com/?ref=48106

No years of therapy.

No weeks of training.

Are you ready to enjoy total change, and access the NLP Secret for yourself?

SPIRITUAL AWAKENING

▶BEYOND CONSCIOUSNESS (Steve G. Jones) [324]

Beyond Consciousness: 8 Subconscious Techniques to Change Your Life is a new program that combines the power of hypnosis, lucid dreaming, meditation, astral projection, astral sex, the Third Eye, and even the Akashic Records to bring peace, clarity, balance and happiness back into any person's life.

To put it simply, if you are experiencing any kind of stress, negativity or imbalance right now, you can use this program to eliminate these negativities from your life so you can be happier and more satisfied with life.

---

[324] http://b3d6b5p6knlisxelmhubvr3q9u.hop.clickbank.net/

Living The ED Principles

If your problems have been weighing you down, now is the time to throw away those heavy boulders that you have been carrying and *fly* to the heights of the Akashic Records and astral realms.

Today marks the beginning of your new life, with this 8-part audio training, available for immediate download as mp3 audio files, and a PDF transcript of all 8 modules.

▶ THE AWAKENING COURSE (Joe Vitale) [325]

This Awakening Course will take you on a magical journey through the four stages of awakening.

During your adventure, Joe will instruct you on the pitfalls and practices of each stage before finally leading you into the fourth and final stage of complete awakening; a place rarely described.

▶ THE SOUL JOURNEY [326]

---

[325] http://cbe2aambnanltyf7bvodv-gl48.hop.clickbank.net/
[326] http://www.thesouljourney.com/?a_aid–195

Living The ED Principles

People everywhere are searching for well-being (meaning, purpose, fulfillment, health and happiness). For life to be good, we need to feel useful and appreciated.

Taking a spiritual growth journey called *The Soul Journey* will enable you to grasp the bigger picture of who you are. You will discover how to distinguish your personality from soul. You will learn practical ways to develop and express soul for a life of meaning and purpose.

In changing your consciousness, you will change your life.

SUBLIMINALS

▶CREATIVE VISUALIZATION WITH SUBLIMINAL SUGGESTIONS: POWER MIND SERIES (Nelson Berry) [327]

▶MASTER MANIFESTER SUBLIMINAL MESSAGES VIDEO SERIES(Nelson Berry) [328]

---

[327] http://1e5355mzeappftal64rk-1bma0.hop.clickbank.net/
[328] http://a65c73m-limmszfqw1nj55ey38.hop.clickbank.net/

Living The ED Principles

▶ SUBLIMINAL HEALTH AND FITNESS (Nelson Berry) [329]

▶ SUBLIMINAL MESSAGES EXTREME (Nelson Berry) [330]

▶ SUBLIMINAL STUDIO (Bradley Thompson) [331]

Those who have studied subliminal messaging believe it is powerful and effective; this is why the CIA invested millions in subliminal messaging research way back in the 1950's. The technology was expanded in the 60's following research studies by William Bryan Key, Vance Packard, and Eldon Taylor, all suggesting that subliminals are a highly effective method of influencing thought.

Subliminal messaging is a method of sending commands directly to the subconscious mind, bypassing the more critical conscious; the subconscious mind quickly absorbs and acts on these commands.

---

[329] http://93af3zl6nijrmuecx9pg-fjz11.hop.clickbank.net/
[330] http://272c0xn6ckihtr5i460hy46od4.hop.clickbank.net/
[331] http://www.subliminal-studio.com/?ref-48106

Living The ED Principles

Anthony Robbins and Tiger Woods both claim that subliminals are the key to their success.

Ask yourself these questions ……

[1] Do you find mass produced subliminal CDs effective?

[2] Do you trust the subliminal tapes/CDs you buy?

[3] Do you sometimes want subliminal recordings for topics that most CDs do not cover?

There is a simple solution.

If you are using a Windows PC with a soundcard, then you already have all the equipment you need.

Just add the powerful *Subliminal Studio* and you will learn exactly how to create your own subliminal tapes, CDs and MP3s, virtually unheard of in the retail world.

The software CD includes: [1] *Developing Your Own Subliminal-Studio* booklet with60 pages of exclusive information guiding you through the process of creating your own subliminal recordings, step-by-step, [2] over three hours of royalty-free relaxation music, [3] 20 pre-recorded subliminal CD scripts, [4] two and a half hours of nature sounds, also royalty free, [5] over two and a half hours of expertly created binaural beats, [6] highly sought after silent subliminal script, and [7] trial version of Adobe Audition for compiling your own subliminal recordings.

▶THE INTELLIGENT WARRIOR SUBLIMINAL VIDEO SERIES (Nelson Berry) [332]

TRILIMINALS

▶QUANTUM TRILIMINALS (with TMM) [333] [334] [335] [336]

▶EFFORTLESS PROSPERITY [337] is Morry's latest, truly amazing, program.

---

[332] http://d21947n2mcklumdm64rd41fubs.hop.clickbank.net/
[333] http://www.themorrymethod.com/tmm.php?id=14
[334] http://quantumtriliminalsuccess.com/Teleseminar2.htm
[335] http://quantumtriliminals.com/trial.htm
[336] http://quantum-mind-power-system.com/fp2/index.html
[337] http://339150jaf8wnpr27iex9zn3k4e.hop.clickbank.net/

Living The ED Principles

Given that one has the power to change their thoughts at any time, so, too, does this change one's outlook (viewpoint, mindset, perception, paradigm) on their reality.

This means that when you are able to change your thinking (courtesy of your brain), so, too, does it change your life. [338]

No matter how you may be struggling to turn your current circumstances around or improve your lot in life, there *is* a powerful secret that actually changes your brain from a place of confusion, discouragement, or negativity, into a powerful vibrational force that will change your life; in fact, scientific research actually proves this to be true.

In summation, the formula to a life of prosperity (peace of mind, emotional well-being, happiness, financial freedom) and abundance is far simpler than most people can possibly imagine.

---

[338] http://effortlessprosperityprogram.com/wp/ep-forgiveness/

About the Author

Michele Doucette is webmistress of Portals of Spirit, a spirituality website whereby one will find links to categories of interest from Angels to Zen, books of spiritual resonance, videos and documentaries. In addition, she holds a Crystal Healing Practitioner diploma (Stonebridge College in the UK) and is guardian to many from the mineral kingdom.

As a Level 2 Reiki Practitioner, she sends long distance Reiki to those who make the request, claiming only to be a channeler of the Universal Energy, thereby allowing the individual(s) in question to heal themselves.

She is the author of spiritual/metaphysical works; namely, [1] _The Ultimate Enlightenment For 2012: All We Need Is Ourselves_, a book that was nominated for the AllBooks Review Best Inspirational Book of 2011, [2] _Turn Off The TV: Turn On Your Mind_, [3] _Veracity At Its Best_, [4] _The Collective: Essays on Reality_ (a composition of essays in relation to the Matrix), [5] _Sleepers Awaken: The Time Is Now To Consciously Create Your Own Reality_, [6] _Healing_ the Planet and Ourselves: How To Raise Your Vibration, [7] You Are Everything: Everything Is You, [8] The Awakening of Humanity: A Foremost Necessity, [9] The Cosmos of The Soul: A Spiritual Biography, [10] Getting Out Of Our Own Way: Love Is The Only Answer, [11] Living The Jedi Way, [12] Vicarius Christi: The Vicar of Christ, [13] A Metaphysics Primer: Changing From The Inside Out and [14] The Cosmos of The Soul II: Messages all of which have been published through St. Clair Publications.

In addition, she has written another volume that deals solely with crystals, aptly entitled The Wisdom of Crystals.

The author of A Travel in Time to Grand Pré, this is a visionary metaphysical novel that historically ties the descendants of Yeshua (Jesus) to modern day Nova Scotia.

As shared by a reviewer, Veracity At Its Best "constructs the context for the spiritual message" imparted in A Travel in Time to Grand Pré.

Against the backdrop of 1754 Acadie, this novel, an alchemical tale of time travel, romance and intrigue, from Henry Sinclair to the Merovingians, from the Cathari treasure at Montségur to the Knights Templar, also blends French Acadian history with current DNA testing.

Together with the words of Yeshua as spoken at the height of his ministry, A Travel in Time to Grand Pré has the potential to inspire others; for it is herein that we learn how individuals can find their way, their truth(s), so as to live their lives to the fullest.

Several years in the making, she was also driven to write Back Home With Evangeline, the sequel. It is here that Madeleine and Michel find themselves back in the twentieth century with a message that must be shared with the world. So, too, and even more importantly, must the message be lived, and experienced, by one and all.

She is also the author of Time Will Tell, a uniquely moving tale that begins in the present day before weaving its way backward through time to connect a glowing thread of historic discoveries.

Courtesy of past-life regression, Michaela (Dr. Mike) Callaghan, a brilliant metaphysical scientist, in the twenty-first century, discovers that she lived as a young, noble, Cathari herbalist healer, in the Languedoc area of France, during a time when political change was in the air.

When not working as a Special Education teacher, she continues to read, research and write, exploring her personal genealogies, all of which constitute her passion.

In the words of the Dalai Lama … *In order to be happy, one must first possess inner contentment; and inner contentment cannot come from having all we want; rather it comes from having and appreciating all we have.*

www.ingramcontent.com/pod-product-compliance
Lightning Source LLC
Chambersburg PA
CBHW071648090426
42738CB00009B/1463